D0330932

HENRY FIELDING'S TOM JONES

THE NOVELIST AS MORAL PHILOSOPHER

TEXT AND CONTEXT

Editors

ARNOLD KETTLE
Professor of Literature
Open University

and

A. K. THORLBY
Professor of Comparative Literature
University of Sussex

◆

BERNARD HARRISON
Henry Fielding's Tom Jones:
The Novelist as Moral Philosopher

JEREMY HAWTHORN
Virginia Woolf's Mrs Dalloway:
A Study in Alienation

LAURENCE LERNER
Thomas Hardy's The Mayor of Casterbridge:
Tragedy or Social History?

Other Titles in Preparation

HENRY FIELDING'S TOM JONES

THE NOVELIST
AS MORAL PHILOSOPHER

Bernard Harrison

Reader in Philosophy in
The University of Sussex

SUSSEX UNIVERSITY PRESS

1975

Randall Library UNC-W

Published for
SUSSEX UNIVERSITY PRESS

BY

Chatto & Windus Ltd
40 William IV Street
London WC2N 4DF

*

Clarke, Irwin & Co Ltd
Toronto

All rights reserved. No part of this
publication may be reproduced, stored
in a retrieval system, or transmitted in
any form, or by any means, electronic,
mechanical, photocopying, recording or
otherwise, without the prior permission
of Chatto & Windus Ltd.

Hardback ISBN 0 85621 044 7

Paperback ISBN 0 85621 045 5

© Bernard Harrison 1975

Printed in Great Britain by
Cox & Wyman Ltd,
London, Fakenham and Reading

PR3454
.H7
.H28

For
Eva, Kate, David

163032

CONTENTS

CONTENTS

PREFACE

This book owes much to the criticism and encouragement of my friends A. D. Nuttall, Stephen Medcalf, A. A. H. Inglis, Gabriel Josipovici, Roy Edgley, B. L. Gibbs and Stephen Prickett, with all of whom I discussed aspects of it at one time or another, while some had the patience and kindness to follow the evolution of its ideas over several years. Chief among the latter is my wife Dorothy, whose observations on Fielding were what first led me to read him.

The book began life as a paper which I read in November 1971 to a group of philosophers and literary critics which meets occasionally at Sussex: a later draft of this appeared in *Radical Philosophy*, No. 6, Winter 1973, under the title 'Fielding and the Moralists'. Parts of Chapters 1–3 were read in May 1974 to a weekend conference on philosophy and literature and profited from the subsequent discussion.

I am at a loss to say whether what the book contains is 'philosophy' or 'literary criticism': I hope it is both, and that they are fused into one substance. It is certainly not my intention to reduce critical questions to philosophical ones, or to 'mine' literature for philosophically interesting generalities. If there is rather a lot of philosophy in the book, it is because I think the discussion of such matters essential if we are to arrive at an adequate reading of Fielding; but that in turn is because Fielding seems to me, contrary to common opinion, a writer of considerable philosophical interest. I hope that moral philosophers, as well as critics, will find things in the book to interest them. But in the sense that I am primarily concerned with the question how Fielding should be read, my intentions are those of a literary critic. To that end I have tried to restrain, up to a point, the philosopher's love of abstract generality for its own sake.

Kingston near Lewes, Sussex.

At the head of these [writers of fiction] we must, for many reasons, place Henry Fielding, one of the most motley of Literary characters . . . He was the author of a romance, entitled 'The history of Joseph Andrews', and of another, 'The Foundling, or the history of Tom Jones', a book seemingly intended to sap the foundation of that morality which it is the duty of parents and all public instructors to inculcate in the minds of young people, by teaching that virtue upon principle is imposture, that generous qualities alone constitute true worth, and that a young man may love and be loved, and at the same time associate with the loosest women. His morality, in respect that it resolves virtue into good affections, in contradiction to moral obligation and a sense of duty, is that of Lord Shaftesbury vulgarised, and is a system of excellent use in palliating the vices most injurious to society. He was the inventor of that cant-phrase goodness of heart, which is every day used as a substitute for probity, and means little more than the virtue of a horse or a dog : in short, he has done more towards corrupting the rising generation than any writer we know of.

– Sir John Hawkins, from *The Works of Samuel Johnson,*
1787, i, 214–15.

And now, my friend, I take this opportunity (as I shall have no other) of heartily wishing thee well . . . I question not but thou hast been told, among other stories of me, that thou wast to travel with a very scurrilous fellow; but whoever told thee so did me an injury. No man detests and despises scurrility more than myself; nor hath any man more reason; for none hath ever been treated with more; and what is a very sad fate, I have had some of the abusive writings of those very men fathered upon me, who, in other of their works, have abused me themselves with the utmost virulence.

All these works, however, I am well convinced, will be dead long before this page shall offer itself to thy perusal; for however short the period may be of my own performances, they will most probably outlive their own infirm author, and the weakly productions of his abusive contemporaries.

– Henry Fielding, from *Tom Jones*, preamble to Book XVIII.

I

THE CASE AGAINST FIELDING

I

The English, whose idea of moral seriousness was, and is still, formed upon the model of the minor dissenting clergy, have never thought Fielding a very serious writer, nor *Tom Jones* a very serious book. In brief, *Tom Jones* has been more loved than admired. It is very funny, and it has a plot of triumphantly absurd complexity. Its characters have long passed as jolly, wholesome and picaresque. It abounds in bloodily robust comic incident of the sort which is as diverting to read about within comfortable reach of port and nuts as it would be disagreeable to experience in real life. Its hero is a fine, well set up young fellow, full of lovable human frailties, and its heroine is beautiful, tender and (as is well) forgiving. Hence the common reputation of the book as a Jolly Good Read and a sort of portable Merrie England.

Against this genial, if trivialising, estimate of Fielding's book must be set a long and tenacious tradition of adverse criticism according to which *Tom Jones* is not so much morally trivial as morally frivolous and corrupting. Johnson could not bear the book.

> I never saw Johnson really angry with me but once, and his displeasure did him so much honour that I loved him the better for it. I alluded rather flippantly, I fear, to some witty passage in Tom Jones: he replied, 'I am shocked to hear you quote from so vicious a book. I am sorry to hear you have read it; a confession which no modest lady should ever make. I scarcely know a more corrupt work.'[1]

Why this vehemence? It is not at all explained, I think, by the immodest *subject-matter* of some parts of the book. The subject-matter with which Richardson, Johnson's literary hero, overwhelmingly concerns himself is seduction and attempted seduction: *Pamela* contains scenes of sexual bullying and

[1] Hannah More, letter to a sister, 1780, *Memoirs of the Life and Correspondence of Mrs. Hannah More*, 1834, i, 168.

attempted rape far more unpleasant than anything in *Tom Jones*. We know that Johnson, in common with others of Fielding's Richardsonian critics, thought Fielding's characters 'low'. (Boswell. 'Will you not allow, Sir, that he draws very natural pictures of human life?' Johnson. 'Why Sir, it is of very low life. Richardson used to say, that had he not known who Fielding was, he should have believed it was an ostler.'[2]) But this gets us very little further. Johnson's thunders are not explained by the fact that Fielding sometimes depicts the lives of the lower orders. Richardson does as much. And besides 'low' is here clearly functioning in part as a moral, and not merely as a social epithet: had Johnson lived nowadays he would have said 'squalid'. But the nature of the squalor Johnson perceived in Fielding remains so far unexplained.

Again, Johnson thought Fielding incapable of depicting character in any profound way. 'In comparing those two writers, he used this expression: "that there was as great a difference between them as between a man who knew how a watch was made, and a man who could tell the hour by looking on the dial-plate." This was a short and figurative state of his distinction between drawing characters of nature and characters of manners.'[3]

And, finally, we know that 'Johnson used to quote with approbation a saying of Richardson's, "that the virtues of Fielding's heroes were the vices of a truly good man".'[4]

Diverse as they are, these judgements are not, I think, unconnected: the various charges, of viciousness, of 'lowness', of inability to depict character, are fragments of a single critical case against Fielding. The nub of the case is to be found in Hawkins' celebrated piece of invective:

> . . . a book seemingly intended to sap the foundation of that morality which it is the duty of parents and all public instructors to inculcate in the minds of young people, by teaching that virtue upon principle is imposture, that generous qualities alone constitute true worth, and that a young man

[2] James Boswell, *Life of Johnson*, ed. G. B. Hill and L. F. Powell (1934), ii, 173–5.

[3] *Op. cit.* pp. 48–9.

[4] *ibid.*

may love and be loved, and at the same time associate with the loosest women. His morality, in respect that it resolves virtue into good affections, in contradiction to moral obligation and a sense of duty, is that of Lord Shaftesbury vulgarised, and is a system of excellent use in palliating the vices most injurious to society. He was the inventor of that cant-phrase goodness of heart, which is every day used as a substitute for probity, and means little more than the virtue of a horse or a dog . . .

Hawkins' fundamental accusation, interestingly enough, is that Fielding is *philosophically* naïve: naïve about the general nature of morality. His error is to hold that virtue is the same thing as warmheartedness. Hawkins sees two things wrong with this. The first is that warmheartedness is a poor guide to right action. Casual warmth of affection leads as easily to whoring as to love: Fielding, he thinks, seems to be unaware of this, or worse, to suppose that it does not matter. The second objection is, if anything, even more damaging. It is that saying that a man is goodhearted says nothing at all about whether or not he is virtuous. For goodheartedness, like good temper, is merely a natural disposition: it is not intrinsically, though it may on occasion be, the outcome of deliberate and conscientious moral choice, and so it does not in itself deserve moral praise. Horses and dogs may, like the genial man, be sociable and amenable in temper, but we do not for that reason suppose them to be moral creatures. Morality is 'obligation and a sense of duty'; it is precisely the capacity to submit all the natural impulses, including on occasion geniality or good heartedness itself, to the rule of a willed and consciously chosen principle.

It is tempting nowadays to dismiss Hawkins as a moralising old woman, but we should resist this temptation. For one thing he is in good philosophical company, notably that of Kant. For another, his blunt and simple arguments have *prima facie*, much force. Indeed, I think it is only through taking such arguments seriously that one can come at a full understanding of Fielding's moral position, or of the nature and function of irony in his work, or of the nature of his art as a novelist.

Certainly Hawkins' arguments illuminate Johnson's charges of 'viciousness' and 'lowness'. If Hawkins is right, Fielding is

13

the defender of a thoroughly specious and shoddy moral latitudinarianism. Everything that is difficult and testing about the moral life is mocked or pushed to one side by an evasive rhetoric of benevolence. The 'lowness' of the book consists in its mock-heroic celebration of the adventures and ultimate rise to fortune of a hero who not only pursues his career on the margins of decent society but pursues it without regard, or at best with an equivocal lip-service paid, to any moral standard tougher or more demanding than the casual benevolence of the alehouse or the sporting party. It is vicious because the very skill with which it devalues the elements of struggle and self-analysis in a virtuous life makes it in the end no more than a rakes' charter.

We cannot evade this criticism by taking refuge in the idea that moral considerations are irrelevant to literature. For Hawkins' moral objections lead directly to a consideration of the supposed formal defects of the book, the chief of which concerns the way in which exploration of character is apparently subordinated to comic elaboration of plot. For, seen from this point of view, the eponymous hero of the book must appear as no more than a genial spiv, whose generosity is made to appear to outweigh the moral weakness and equivocation which it masks only because the artificial contrivances of Fielding's plot protect his characters from suffering the consequences of their actions. Nothing but the revelation of Bridget Allworthy's relationship with Mr Summer saves Tom from having committed incest; nothing but the fortuitous strength of Mr Fitzpatrick's constitution saves him from the gallows. Thus Frank Kermode:

(Tom) represents a hot-blooded version of Allworthy; he stands for what was for Fielding a desirable vital compromise between excellent principles and the plenary and immediate operation of natural instinct. In so far as the interest theme is not a merely theatrical peripeteia, it must stand as the crisis of this alliance of incompatibles. In this instance the uninhibited demonstration of sexual prowess does not ultimately escape with a reproof from an understanding lover, a muff on the bed; it is suddenly confronted with the awful judgement of principle exalted into taboo. This is, one might think, the contrivance (*un*contrived) of a devoted moralist. He has produced a situation which, as the whole European tradition instructs us, is tragic . . . Fielding's situation can only be evaded by an unethical stroke of good luck; and this is what Fielding, not without a parade of 'technical' dexterity, offers. Now the flesh and the spirit of Jones are matters of common observation; but his good luck is not. Fielding the moralist completely evades the only genuinely crucial test that confronts his hero as a moral being, in the whole course of his adventures. The Comic Spirit has intervened, as usual theatrically, to solve what is essentially a theatrically over-simple dualism of character.[5]

The result of all this plotting is that action is divorced from character. The events of the book are never allowed to flow, as they do in Richardson, from the inner lives of the characters. 'Fielding is the epic writer, Richardson the dramatic. Richardson creates by projecting himself imaginatively into his characters, who create the developing situation. In Fielding it is our direct experience of the author's vision that is all important, and he is always between the reader and the action.'[6]

Fielding's preference for what Johnson called 'characters of manners' over 'characters of nature' thus appears, on this view, as the necessary consequence of his espousal of a naïve benevolism. In other words, the necessity of maintaining a crude moral philosophy as the underlying 'message' of the novel meant that Fielding could not seriously embark upon a naturalistic exploration of character, action, and inner life, if the comic surface of the novel was to be maintained, or for that matter if the essential shoddiness of Fielding's underlying conception of morality as goodheartedness was not to be exposed. The 'lowness' and 'viciousness' of *Tom Jones*, and the brilliance of

[5] Frank Kermode, 'Richardson and Fielding', *Cambridge Journal*, 4 (1950), 106–14. I am not sure whether Professor Kermode would any longer wish to defend the views he expressed in this paper: I think it quite likely that he would not. My reason for devoting so much space in what follows to arguing against what he says there is not that I wish to engage in polemical controversy against an opponent safely distanced in time: it is simply that I have been unable to find any more recent paper which so brilliantly, incisively and clearly states the nub of the Johnsonian case against Fielding.

[6] Mark Kincaid-Weekes, *Samuel Richardson, Dramatic Novelist*, London, Methuen, 1973, p. 467.

technical contrivance by means of which Fielding bestows a sur-face animation upon 'characters of manners' through the agency of an externally imposed plot and a suffocatingly ubiquitous authorial presence can thus indeed, as we might expect from the juxtaposition of these grounds of attack in the scattered remains of Johnson's orally delivered criticism, be seen as intrinsically connected. The connexion is forged when we see them as both springing equally from the theoretical inadequacy of the morality of 'goodness of heart' to the description of the actual moral complexities of human life.

Thus, it seems, the heart of the case brought against Fielding by his Richardsonian contemporaries lies in Hawkins' root charge of philosophical naïveté: 'his morality . . . is that of Lord Shaftesbury vulgarised.' Fielding's fundamental fault, on this account, was that he blurred the distinction between the will and the passions; between principle and impulse. A similar charge of philosophical simple-mindedness is at the heart of the article by Frank Kermode which I quoted earlier.

There is nothing intellectualistist about the moral criteria of the good heart. They come, in the long run, to common sense, which in this context is a supposedly instinctive under-standing on the part of both reader and writer of Right and Wrong. Fielding was perfectly well aware that, given the validity of his method, he had to demand of the reader an identity of interest and point of view with his own. 'The author must have a good heart and feel what he expects his reader to feel' (*Tom Jones*, 1). Thus Fielding explicitly re-quires his reader to possess the Good Heart. One would there-fore not expect to find in Fielding, at any rate in the normal course, any critical examination or reasoned extension of the moral criteria, though it is true that in *Amelia* he is con-cerned with the direct examination of the practical menace involved by (*sic*) certain contemporary moral and psycho-logical beliefs. But in *Amelia*, the effect is to emphasise all the more heavily the purely common-sense and unphilosophical nature of the normal Good Heart, and further to establish that dissociation of character and conduct which Coleridge so acutely remarked and applauded in Tom Jones.[7]

[7] Frank Kermode, *op. cit.* p. 109.

Moral intuitionism, the theory that we perceive the difference between right and wrong through the operation of a moral sense, is a doctrine which recurs perennially in English philosophy. It is true that Shaftesbury held certain views of this general sort, and true too that in its least sophisticated forms moral intuitionism amounts to no more than an appeal to the moral common sense of the average man. If this is what Fielding means by 'Goodness of Heart', then all the labours of irony and technical brilliance of plotting will indeed be needed to represent such simplicities as profundities, and will equally inevitably be thrown away. Kermode drives the point home:

> Given Fielding's 'point of view', you cannot let events 'talk' – you are too busy plotting them, they are too *bien faite*, they forfeit morality to Sardoodledom. Or if you leave them unplotted and merely recorded, you have to risk the fact that their unadorned significance may be less to the reader than to you – or even something quite different. And so you must assert your own standards. If these are the standards and yours is the sensibility of *l'homme moyen sensuel*, then your irony will flicker, however brilliantly, against the dreary background of the decent chap – in Fielding's case, against a genuinely good-humoured, high-spirited, humane, orthodox gentleman of the eighteenth century. And no matter how delightful that may be, one questions whether the *value* of the product – and by this is meant not its historical value or its readability but its essential moral value – is equivalent to that of a less accomplished, less urbane, less sociable, less witty writer, Richardson, who chose not to be God's spy, but rather to draw his breath in pain and tell the story.[8]

II

And yet . . . and yet. We have before us three charges against Fielding: moral evasiveness; the naïveté of the supposedly Shaftesburian moral pieties from which the evasiveness is alleged to spring; and an allegorist's predilection for wooden characters each defined once and for all in terms of a few static traits of character, incapable of development because devoid of

[8] *ibid*, p. 114.

any properly realised inner-life, and so incapable of *generating* the events of the novel, which must in consequence be stage-managed by the author through the agency of clockwork intricacies of plot. If the second charge is the fundamental one, the purely literary case against Fielding rests upon the third. The implication of the charge is that Fielding is not a *novelist* at all, but at most a writer of moral allegories or fables, since he is simply not interested in the exploration of the relationships between character and conduct which constitutes the main business of the serious novelist.

Fielding's own explanations of his intentions lend some credence to this claim. 'I declare once and for all, I describe not men but manners; not an individual but a species,' he says in the preface to Book 3 of *Joseph Andrews*. The remark has some-times been taken as an avowal of the justice of Johnson's criti-cism: 'describing manners' sounds much like describing the overt behaviour of men and neglecting their inner life – describing the dial-plate of the watch rather than its works. But I am not sure that Fielding is really delivering himself into Johnson's hands. Certainly Coleridge found more in Fielding than descriptions of manners. On the flyleaf of volume IV of his edition of *Tom Jones*[9] he wrote:

> If I want a servant or mechanic, I wish to know what he *does* – but of a Friend, I must know what he *is*. And in no writer is this momentous distinction so finely brought forward as by Fielding. We do not care what Blifil *does* – the *deed*, as separate from the agent, may be good or ill – but Blifil *is* a villain – and we feel him to be so, from the very moment he, the boy Blifil, restored Sophia's poor captive bird to its native and rightful liberty.

Kermode speaks of 'that dissociation of character and con-duct which Coleridge so acutely remarked and applauded in *Tom Jones*', and continues :

> It seemed to Coleridge admirable that we are given a highly favourable view of Jones' character in spite of his revealed conduct; and he rightly suggested that Fielding stressed this dissociation when he made Blifil perform, when

[9] Now in the British Museum.

he released Sophia's bird, a commendable act for despicable motives. What seems less certain is that this species of observation is not mere grist to Johnson's mill.[10]

Here, I think, Kermode overstates his case, in the process obscuring both the point of Coleridge's defence and the point of Johnson's criticism. Johnson saw in Fielding's characters only dial-plates with no clockwork behind them. To say this is to say that they *are* no more than their recorded overt behaviour. This is a fair description of 'characters of manners' or of allegory in the crudest sense. Sir Fopling Fribble is a fop and a frivol because he behaves like one, with comic or wearisome consistency. We know he is a fop because *all* we know about him is that he behaves like one: that is why he is a character of manners and why it would be absurd to raise the question of what he *is* as against what he *does*. It is misleading, now, to describe what Johnson is objecting to in Fielding as the dissociation of 'character from conduct'. It is clear enough why Kermode does this. He has firmly fixed in his mind that vision of what a novel is which requires that the conduct of characters should always flow from, in the sense of being fully explicable in terms of, inner life: the underlying web of motives, predilections, traits of character, moral choices, images, interpretations, fears, fantasies, and so on. Johnson is indeed saying that this does not happen in Fielding, but the reason Johnson assigns for its not happening is not that Fielding's characters have two aspects – 'character' and 'conduct', which are dissociated – but that they have only one aspect, namely conduct or 'manners', which has therefore perforce to do duty for 'character' in the sense of inwardness, as well. Johnson is saying, in other words, that Fielding's characters' character *is* their conduct, and that that is why they are (as Johnson evidently thought) so wooden and static.

It follows that Coleridge's comment is *not* mere grist to Johnson's mill. For Coleridge is saying (and Kermode in some sense or other seems to want to agree with him) that it is possible to distinguish in the case of Fielding's characters (or some of them) between what they *do* and what they *are*. But if we can do that then they cannot (or cannot all) be 'characters of manners' in

[10] Kermode, *op. cit.* p. 109.

the sense which Johnson intended. Kermode's criticism is not, then, Johnsonian in provenance, and must be considered separately. It is that being and doing are separate and distinct in Fielding, but are 'dissociated'.

'Dissociation', of course, is Kermode's term, not Coleridge's. Coleridge implies that we *know* what Fielding's characters are, as distinct from what they do, though later he modifies it to 'feel'. Whether we 'know' or 'feel' such a difference, the knowing or feeling (unless, of course, Coleridge is just reading something into Fielding), must be under Fielding's control: the question is, how? Kermode and Johnson are both right, obviously, that in Fielding being and doing are not often connected, as they often are in Richardson, by what we know of a character's inner-consciousness: Tom's soliloquies are an exception, but Coleridge found these forced and unnatural,[11] and perhaps he was right. Kermode concludes, in effect, that if the description of consciousness is not there to hold being and doing together, nothing holds them together: they are 'dissociated'. But in that case, how do we know – or why do we feel – that 'Blifil *is* a villain'? Kermode suggests *en passant* that it is because Fielding explicitly tells us so: 'It seemed to Coleridge admirable that *we are given* a highly favourable view of Jones' character in spite of his revealed conduct.' (My italics.) This leans upon a widespread critical stereotype (fostered by Fielding's love of didactic comment and his philosophical or mock-philosophical prefaces to the books of *Tom Jones*) of Fielding the old bore, ever intrusively at his reader's elbow, never willing to let the action of the novel speak for itself, forced to tell you explicitly what his characters are inwardly like because he cannot allow their inwardness to be displayed through their actions without subverting both his mechanical plot and his wearisome moral didacticism. But I don't think, as we shall see later, that much textual support can be found for this stereotype as a solution to the problem with which Coleridge's comment confronts us. At the point at which, according to Coleridge, we feel first that Blifil is a scoundrel (the episode of the caged bird), authorial comment is as strikingly absent as is the revelation of inner consciousness: the characters just talk.

[11] *See Coleridge, Select Poetry and Prose*, ed. Stephen Potter, Nonesuch Press 1962, p. 357.

20

Empson, in an invaluable essay,[12] comes close to the point:

> I take it he refused to believe that the 'inside' of a person's mind (as given by Richardson in a letter, perhaps) is much use for telling you the real source of his motives. You learn that from what he does, and therefore a novelist ought to devise an illustrative plot.

I think, in fact, that Empson is at the heart of the matter here, but like much else in his essay what he says is terse and obscure: it leaves us wondering *how* exactly we learn the real source of a person's motives from what he does (and what exactly an 'illustrative plot' is); just as Coleridge leaves us wondering how, exactly, we do learn what Blifil *'is'*.

III

Just as obscure doubts seem to be in order about the naïveté of Fielding's treatment of character, so obscure doubts are abroad about his philosophical naïveté. This is important because, as I have tried to show, it is on the putative shallowness and facility of Fielding's general moral outlook that the charge of 'lowness' must rest, if it is to be a serious charge. In general Fielding's more eminent critics in the eighteenth century do push the charge in this direction, towards identifying 'lowness' with moral frivolity and superficiality – a cheapjack disregard for principle, moral struggle and moral self-analysis – while the minor ones concentrate on the alleged lewdness of the novels, supplemented by accusations of loose living against Fielding himself.

What is beyond doubt is that there is an enormous amount of philosophical and quasi-philosophical discussion of morality in Fielding, and that Fielding was well-read in both moral philosophy and moral theology. Moreover, what one might call the 'small print' of philosophical discussion sometimes erupts into Fielding's work in a way which would hardly be compatible with a slight or superficial acquaintance with such matters. In *Amelia* the central error which Booth finally renounces to the delight of the good Dr Harrison is identified with Hobbes'

[12] William Empson, 'Tom Jones' in *Fielding*, ed. Ronald Paulson, Prentice-Hall, 1962, p. 135.

doctrine that 'will is the last appetite of deliberation' (that we always act in accordance with our strongest desire). It does not take philosophical genius to see that this apparently abstruse and arid bit of rational psychology is important, and that it is in fact the central pillar of philosophical egoism; but it does take close reading and an acute philosophical intelligence.

The range of philosophical and theological influences on Fielding has been made clear by much recent criticism. Martin Battestin's book, *The Moral Basis of Fielding's Art*,[13] for example, explores in admirable detail the nature of Fielding's conception of Christian morality, and its debt to the latitudinarian moral theology of Barrow, Tillotson, Clarke and Hoadly. But scholarly literary history of this sort, while invaluable, has certain limitations. Because it concentrates on tracing the influences on a writer it is not very well adapted to showing what he has made of them. An idea is not a self-contained item of negotiable intellectual currency : it does not have a settled value and significance inscribed upon it like a banknote or a share-certificate. The life of ideas is in systems of thought, and the same idea may take on a radically different weight and significance when transferred from one such system to another. This is something which influence-tracing as an activity undervalues: it is subject to an inevitable temptation to suppose that when we have assembled the influences bearing upon a writer we have understood his mind; whereas what we have done is often merely to assemble the materials upon which his mind worked to produce a structure yet to be comprehended. The temptation, in short, is always to regard the recipient of an older idea as a passive exponent of it, and to reserve originality for the original begetter, neglecting the truth that thought is not a matter of juxtaposing but of articulating ideas, and that originality in thought consists as much in the articulation as in the materials articulated.

Perhaps not unnaturally, therefore, the modern interest in the philosophical sources of Fielding's thought has tended, if anything, to reinforce Hawkins' estimate of Fielding as an intellectually feeble and imitative writer. Thus, for example, Battestin summarises Fielding's ethics like this:

[13] Martin C. Battestin, *The Moral Basis of Fielding's Art, A Study of 'Joseph Andrews'*, Wesleyan University Press, 1959.

22

To recapitulate, then, Fielding's view of human nature generally coincided with that of the latitudinarians in its overall optimism. Because of his belief in the theory of a predominant passion, as well as his Christian conception of man's weakness since the Fall, he recognises that true good nature is rare. With Isaac Barrow and his own Harrison, however, he affirmed that man was essentially *capable* of great goodness, if only he were assisted by the institutions of society and persuaded by the powerful incentives of religion to a proper use of his reason and will. On the other hand, the completely moral man, like the heroes of the novels, was by nature compassionate, selfless and benevolent – his heart so open and innocent that its generous impulses needed, for his own sake and that of society, to be directed and controlled by reason. This man, the good-natured man, wanted no other inducement to morality than his own benevolent disposition. His love for humanity naturally expressed itself in acts of charity, the supreme virtue and the sum of religion. Without charity, faith and knowledge and ritual were dead and were insufficient to salvation.[14]

Something has gone wrong here. The amiably *bien pensant* latitudinarian simpleton who emerges from this summary is not recognisable as the savage satirist whose irony Coleridge thought superior to Swift's[15] and whose vision of the corruption masked by moral platitude resembles and on occasion even takes on the accents of Mandeville.[16]

Again W. R. Irwin cites as influences Shaftesbury, Hutcheson, Butler, Whichcote, Pope, and in general the benevolist opposition to Hobbes; in other words, those who believed in benevolence as a fundamental human impulse alongside self-interest, and who believed, moreover, that the exercise of benevolence was compatible with, because an essential means to, the pursuit of true self-interest; having done this he concludes:

[14] Battestin, *op. cit.*, p. 84.
[15] *See* the Nonesuch *Coleridge*, pp. 718–19.
[16] *See*, for example, *An Essay on the Characters of Men*, in V. XV of the Henley *Works*.

To summarise, popular writers of the first half of the eighteenth century, intent on the moral instruction and improvement of their readers, presented under varying names two opposing conceptions – greatness and goodness – which were simplifications of the ethical dualism on which learned speculation centred. Henry Fielding, a competent amateur in philosophy, adopted these popular notions, and in early essays, poems, and dramas developed them . . . into well defined themes . . . Ethically considered then, *Jonathan Wild* is a popular allegorical presentation of a fundamental moral problem.[17]

This is indeed grist to Johnson's mill. It is not just that the dismissive 'a competent amateur in philosophy' echoes Hawkins' '. . . Lord Shaftesbury vulgarised.' It is that the philosophical company in which Irwin places Fielding, if we take Fielding as a mere exponent of similar views, is, with the exception of Butler, not very impressive. The debate about whether men are wholly selfish or also (some of the time) benevolent, and about whether 'morality' in the sense of benevolence is or is not compatible with 'self-interest' in some sense of that obscure term, is certainly far less fundamental than that other controversy whose heights are dominated still by Kant and Hume (and in which Johnson, Hawkins and Richardson side, in effect, with Kant), over whether morality is fundamentally a matter of sentiment, of the impulses of the heart, or whether it consists rather in willed obedience to principle and is in consequence at perpetual odds with impulse. The two controversies of course overlap in places, but the second is radically more fundamental and far-reaching than the first: to assign Fielding to a place in the spectrum of views defined by the first is thus to classify him automatically as relatively negligible from a philosophical point of view.

The most radical defence of Fielding, as a moral theorist, so far as I know, is once again Empson's.

In *Tom Jones* he (Fielding) is expressing a theory about ethics and the ironies are made to interlock with the progress of the demonstration. The titanic plot, which has been

[17] William Robert Irwin, *The Making of Jonathan Wild*, Archon Books, Hampden, Connecticut, 1966.

praised or found tiresome taken alone, was devised to illustrate the theory, and the screws of the engine of his style are engaging the sea. That is, the feeling that he is proving a case is what gives *Tom Jones* its radiance, making it immensely better, I think, than the other two novels (though perhaps there is merely less discovery about proving the sad truths of *Amelia*); it builds up like Euclid. Modern critics seem unable to feel this, apparently because it is forbidden by their aesthetic principles, even when Fielding tells them he is doing it; whereas Dr Johnson and Sir John Hawkins, for example, took it seriously at once, and complained bitterly that the book had an immoral purpose. It certainly becomes more interesting if you attend to its thesis, even if the thesis retains the shimmering mystery of a mirage.[18]

All this is immensely right-headed, it seems to me. The book is nothing without its intellectual framework, and that framework is indeed the clue to the interactions of plot and character. The underlying thesis dominates and directs the systematic patterns of irony which run through the book; and irony, of a very peculiar and intellectually fascinating sort, is the mortar which cements plot to character. Those critics who have found no difference of level between character and action in the book, or who have found separate levels corresponding to what a character *is* and what he *does*, but without any intelligible and systematic connexion between the two, have done so, it seems to me, because they have failed to see that through his use of irony Fielding has gained access to a mode of representation of the interaction of character and conduct altogether different from that other mode – operating through the attempted description of inner consciousness – which informs the aesthetic and technique of the Richardsonian novel. And that, in turn, has something to do with the fact that Fielding, subscribing to a different moral philosophy, subscribes *a fortiori* to a different moral psychology: which takes us back at once to the question of the nature of his theory.

Here Empson is no help. An intellectual construct powerful enough to do what I explicitly and Empson implicitly claim for it cannot for ever be shrouded in 'the shimmering mystery of a

[18] Empson, *op cit.*, p. 125.

mirage'. Elsewhere Empson suggests that the real obstacle to coming clean about the intellectual content of Fielding's theory is the ever-present analytical intransigence of that familiar ogre 'the modern philosopher.'

> [Fielding's] doctrine is thus: 'If good by nature, you can imagine other people's feelings so directly that you have an impulse to act on them as though they were your own; and this is the source of your greatest pleasure as well as of your only genuinely unselfish actions.' A modern philosopher might argue that this makes no difference, but it clearly brings a large practical difference into the suasive effect of the argument of Hobbes, which was what people had thought worth discussing in the first place.[19]

This is not a bad stab at a brief statement of Fielding's doctrine, but it contains, as I shall try to show, serious distortions. It would clearly not take much critical pressure to make the doctrine, as Empson has it here, collapse into the view that being moral comes to no more than natural benevolence and a liking for seeing people happy, which is the very view that Fielding's critics have always found, rightly I think, intellectually naïve.

Moreover Empson grants the *philosophical* inadequacy of Fielding's position as an off-hand aside. 'A modern philosopher would argue that this makes no difference.' This is where I part company with Empson, or rather, want to go further. I don't find Fielding's intellectual position philosophically indefensible. Indeed, I think that, properly stated, it is rather impressive simply from a philosophical point of view, leaving aside the literary power of the vein of irony which it informs and directs. I think that a proper understanding of it is essential to a fully adequate reading of all his work, and of *Tom Jones* in particular. By that I don't mean that nobody has ever understood Fielding at all (though I think few of his readers have in fact read him, as it were, at full stretch). The materials for a reconstruction of Fielding's mind and for the construction of a serious reply to the traditional charges of Richardsonian criticism lie scattered throughout the literature of Fielding criticism. But

[19] Empson, *op. cit.*, pp. 128-9.

scattered they lie, and what I think *is* true is that they can only be united through a reconsideration of Fielding as a moral theorist.

On the principle of setting thieves to catch thieves, this is clearly a task for a literary-minded, or tame, philosopher. And it is in this modest role of Fielding's philosophical bulldog that I shall mainly cast myself in what follows.

But at the same time I have ulterior philosophical motives for an interest in Fielding's moral theory. The dichotomy between Reason and Sentiment, Principle and Impulse, Duty and Pleasure, Thought and Feeling, which came increasingly to dominate the philosophical discussion of morals in the eighteenth century, dominates it, at least in English-speaking philosophy[20] still. The philosophically interesting thing about Fielding is that he is outside this dichotomy. Far from being impaled, as Richardsonians have always argued, upon the horn of the dilemma marked 'Impulse', he has found a way of going between the horns. He has vaulted the bull and is free; and from the standpoint which as a result is made available to us, if we are prepared to work hard enough to see in what it consists, and what has made the vault possible, certain interesting philosophical possibilities open out. Moreover, certain things about the technique of Fielding's kind of novel make it in some ways a more fruitful vehicle for the elaboration of philosophical ideas than explicit philosophical discussion itself. But that point must wait on what is to follow.

[20] Iris Murdoch, in her interesting book *The Sovereignty of Good*, says much the same thing about existentialism.

2

CHARACTER AND CONDUCT

I

The case which Coleridge chose as offering a crucial test of Fielding's power to make us feel the gulf between how a man appears in his public conduct and what he *is*, is the episode in *Tom Jones* (Bk. IV, Ch. 3) in which the young Blifil releases the pet bird which Tom had given to Sophia. Tom tries to coax the bird from a tree and falls into the canal through climbing after it; Sophia weeps; Blifil defends himself on grounds of his having felt a humanitarian pity for the bird, but blames himself on the grounds that, without anyone having noticed in the general confusion, the bird has in fact just been captured by a hawk; Sophia's sobs redouble. The incident gives occasion for a grand casuistical debate between Thwackum and Square: Allworthy takes Blifil's plea of humanitarianism as worthy of serious consideration in balancing it against other aspects of his action; Western dismisses it out of hand as an impudent and pious fraud. All of the important questions about Fielding as a novelist arise and can be discussed, it seems to me, in connexion with this one incident.

Coleridge's claim, I take it, is implicitly that Western is right. Allworthy, with his saintly simplemindedness, and Thwackum and Square with their respective theoretical axes of Shaftesburian rationalism and theological obscurantism to grind, all fail to see for various reasons what is immediately apparent to the commonplace peasant shrewdness of an ignorant and intemperate booby squire. I think this is indeed how Fielding intends us to read the episode, at least on the most general and schematic level; and if, like the rest of Fielding's treatment of Square it tends to count against Hawkins' identification of Fielding as a Shaftesburian, it seems equally to add fuel to Kermode's criticism that Fielding's morality comes down to an implicit trust in the moral instincts of the Common Man: Western is the Common Man on stilts.

But what is it that Coleridge can have seen about Blifil's

action, as Fielding describes it? First of all, I suppose, that Blifil's humanitarianism is oddly limited in its objects. He *says* he feels for the bird what his subsequent utterance makes it quite clear that he does *not* feel for Sophia in her loss.

Master Blifil answered, 'Indeed, uncle, I am very sorry for what I have done; I have been unhappily the occasion of it all. I had Miss Sophia's bird in my hand, and thinking the poor creature languished for liberty, I own I could not forbear giving it what it desired; for I always thought there was something very cruel in confining anything. It seemed to be against the law of nature, by which everything has a right to liberty; nay it is even unchristian, for it is not doing what we would be done by; but if I had imagined Miss Sophia would be so concerned at it, I am sure I never would have done it; nay if I had known what would have happened to the bird itself: for when Master Jones, who climbed up the tree after it, fell into the water, the bird took a second flight, and presently a nasty hawk carried it away.'

This speech, from whichever way one looks at it: as a piece of tongue-in-cheek writing by Fielding at Blifil's expense, or as a piece of inadvertent self-revelation by Blifil, is a little masterpiece, in which successive comic ironies are nested like Chinese boxes. For the first few phrases, up to 'desired', Blifil's words sound like a genuine apology for an act genuinely performed on a sudden impulse of pity for a caged creature. But just when on this interpretation, the speech should stop, it mysteriously continues; more, it turns into a brief sermon; a sermon, moreover, which combines in beautiful balance Shaftesburian pieties about the Law of Nature and the Natural Right to Liberty, manifestly intended as a gesture to Square, and an equally well-turned nod to Thwackum in the shape of a swift exercise in self-justification by derivation from the Golden Rule buttressed by the sombre Gothic edifice of the word 'unchristian'. We then reach the astonishing claim: 'but if I had imagined Miss Sophia would have been so much concerned at it, I am sure I never would have done it . . .' This is altogether too much of a good thing. Someone sensitive enough to have been genuinely moved to release the bird by a sudden impulse of distress at its confinement would surely have been moved a moment later by an equally pressing impulse of distress for the bereaved Sophia, and thus moved to make some apology, perhaps even a tearful apology, for having acted hastily, on impulse, in a genuinely morally complex situation. Now at this point Blifil's whole claim to whatever moral latitude is due to the impulsively generous begins to fall apart. A genuinely impulsively generous person might claim that the flood of pity had momentarily prevented him from recollecting what, had he stopped and reflected for a moment, he would have known well enough (i.e., that Sophia would be distressed), but simple *ignorance* of Sophia's likely reaction is simply not consonant with the character which Blifil is trying to simulate. And when we proceed from this point in the speech to the final disclosure of Tommy's fate in the hawk's talons, all trace of plausibility has fallen away from the sham. For now it is not merely that Blifil is stumbling in the portrayal of certain features of the surface behaviour of a type of character whose real inward springs are altogether obscure to him; rather his own real character is, as it were, now commencing to well up through the cracks in the portrayal. Not so much shame as distress would make the genuinely impulsively generous soul conceal Tommy's fate for as long as possible: Sophia's renewed sobs would be too much to bear. But Master Blifil's sweet treble pipe soars bravely on, encompassing in its flight the final virtuoso meanness of an attempt to shift the blame for Tommy's death on to the dripping and speechless Tom.

> ... *for when Master Jones, who climbed up the tree after it, fell into the water,* the bird took a second flight ...

So much, then, for a first-order account of what is going on in this one speech: I would not have risked boring the reader with such painstaking detail if it were not evident from much published criticism that a very great deal of the detail of Fielding's writing – and his skill as miniaturist of character is not only considerable but, as we shall see, indispensable to his role as philosopher and moralist – is going over the heads, or past the ears of many of his readers.[21]

[21] The myth of Fielding as morally and intellectually feeble but technically brilliant leads to his being read at a gallop for the plot and the action: hence he is seldom read, I suspect, with the close and ruminative attention which

Now for some second-order reflections. The question of Blifil's sincerity turns, if one puts it in the most general terms, on the question whether his professed feelings for the bird cohere morally with the lack of feeling for Sophia manifested by his original action and by the internal logic of the speech which we have just examined. In the marvellously comic bout of casuistry which occupies the succeeding chapter, Square and Thwackum sedulously avoid the awkward question of Blifil's feelings for Sophia. They confine their attention strictly to the question of the moral propriety of freeing caged birds, with Square attributing young Blifil's laudable behaviour to his reverence for the Law of Nature, and Thwackum attributing it to his reverence for the law of God, each resting his case upon their pupil's speech of excuse and justification. Thence the debate proceeds into deeper waters. Allworthy regrets the loss of Sophia's property; Square, by now fully astride the topic, warmly retorts that were 'the dirty consideration of property' to enter into the judgement of great and noble deeds 'the younger Brutus had been accused of ingratitude and the older of patricide'. This is Rousseau before his time, and is too much for Thwackum, who falls with venom upon the heathen Romans and their purported virtues, whereupon the debate at last finds its real topic and dissolves into animated recrimination between the tutors.

In all this, only Western cleaves to the point: what of Sophia?

'Drink about,' says Western, 'Pox of your laws of nature! I don't know what you mean, either of you, by right and wrong. To take away my girl's bird was wrong, in my opinion; and my neighbour Allworthy may do as he pleases; but to encourage boys in such practices, is to breed them up to the gallows.'

And later:

'Pox! You have neither of you mentioned a word of that poor lad who deserves to be commended: to venture breaking his neck to oblige my girl was a generous spirited action: I have learning enough to see that. D—n me, here's Tom's

his work demands and deserves. And that in turn, of course, helps to reinforce the myth.

31

health! I shall love the boy for it the longest day I am to live.'

You can see Western's role in these interventions, if you like, as merely that of the injured father and outraged property owner. And you will, in a way, be right: Fielding gives you warrant for this in Western's response to Square's attack on property.

'So between you both,' says the squire, 'the young gentleman hath been taught to rob my daughter of her bird. I find I must take care of my partridge-mow. I shall have some virtuous religious man or other set all my partridges at liberty.'

Down with Western, the reader, and the modern reader especially, will cry. We all know how to laugh at game-preserving landowners. But the satire here is typically double-edged, and one edge is turned against the moral complacency of the reader. For does not Western's concern for his partridge mow fit naturally with a concern for his daughter's bird? And isn't the justice of that concern the thing that Square and Thwackum keep shuffling out of sight?

It is ironic that this passage has been used to convict Fielding of a naïve belief in the moral infallibility of the unschooled impulses of a generous heart. For let us suppose for the sake of argument that Blifil's impulses had been sound: that he really had released the bird under the pressure of an unbearable pity at its confinement, only to be seized a moment later by remorse at the spectacle of Sophia's tears. Western's observations would still fall with equal justice upon the case. Benevolent impulse (genuine now) would still have led to an act of mean cruelty, performed now in and through the blindness of moral self-absorption. Blifil would qualify for moral latitude but hardly for exoneration: we might sympathise with the *impulse*, indeed, but not with his impulsive*ness*, nor with his callous inattention to the most obvious and immediate consequences of his acts. Considerations of property would, in this case, obviously be a preservative against just such callous moral narcissim. So property is, or can on occasion be, a serious moral consideration, and the way in which its defence is put (with great plausibility) into the mouth of the fool Western should unseat the reader (at least a candid and careful reader) from one of his own moral hobbyhorses.

It is crucial to my point, and Fielding's, that both Thwackum and Square argue not for leniency towards Blifil but for exoneration. If Thwackum were to be believed, Blifil has acted like a juvenile St Francis of Assisi; if Square, he is a budding Brutus to whom no creature is too insignificant to harbour the divine spark of Liberty. The comedy resides not only in the absurd magniloquence of these claims but in the route by which they are arrived at. Thwackum's technique, like Square's, is to assimilate the act of releasing the bird to a favoured principle of action, be it Reverence for the Harmony of Nature or Love of God. If an action can be seen as falling under either principle it is regarded as *de facto* right. Now, of course, as the squabble between Thwackum and Square itself reveals, almost any action can in this sense be assimilated to almost any abstract principle, provided you are careful to avert your eyes from enough of the context in which the action was performed. There is a comic contrast between the show of learning, the phrasemongering, with which Thwackum and Square defend and elaborate their respective principles in abstract terms, and the sedulous disrespect for the concrete detail of actual cases which they display in their indecent haste to appropriate, for the credit of one side or the other in the theoretical quarrel about Nature or God, the choice morsel of Blifil's highmindedness.

Western's interventions, then, are not anti-intellectual *per se*. Fielding is not, in other words, using comic pastiche to devalue thought at the expense of unreasoning impulse. Those who have argued, 'Fielding clearly wishes us to agree with Western about the rights and wrongs of the caged bird episode; Western is a plain, unthinking, impulsive man; therefore Fielding holds the moral impulses of the unthinking plain Englishman to be infallible', have simply missed the point; or rather, a whole series of points. Western's is the uneasy, jerky desperation of the plain man who knows in his bones that the real issues are being slickly begged (he can't quite understand how) by men with far more formal education and verbal fluency than he possesses, and who tries to drag the discussion back to what he obscurely feels to be the point, without any real hope of managing it.

'Well,' says the Squire, 'if it be *nullus bonus*, let us drink about, and talk a little of the state of the nation, or some such discourse that we all understand; for I am sure I don't understand a word of this. It may be learning and sense for all I know: but you shall never persuade me into it.'

II

In short one can see Western as speaking up, however obscurely, not for unreasoning impulse but for intellectual honesty. There really is something intellectually shoddy about Thwackum's and Square's discussion of the case. The reader sees this because Fielding, with the atention to forensic detail which Empson has noticed,[22] has laid the facts before him. But *how* has the reader judged; how has he arrived at the superior level of moral insight from which he can detect the fraud in Thwackum's and Square's learned tergiversations and take Western's part despite Western's manifest inability to do anything but feel obscure moral intuitions and shout? (We are back again to Coleridge's 'we feel him to be so' and to the obvious question ('how?') which Coleridge's aphorism raises.)

Kermode's tradition of Johnsonian criticism answers that the reader has attained no such superior level of moral understanding; it is just that the example has been presented in such a way as to appeal to the unthinking prejudices of the reader, if that reader happens to be *un homme moyen sensuel:* an average decent chap. Such a reader will naturally agree with Fielding and Western in liking Tom (for being a brave little fellow) and disliking Bilfil (for being a budding intellectual who tries to give

---

[22] Empson, *op. cit*, p. 145: 'his conception of a gentleman . . . (was) if anything a literal-minded one. He means by it a person fit to sit on the bench as a magistrate, and naturally such a man needs to know all about the people he is to judge; indeed, the unusual thing about Fielding as a novelist is that he is always ready to consider what he would do if one of his characters came before him on the bench. . . . As to the reader of a novel, Fielding cannot be bothered with him unless he, too, is fit to sit on a magistrate's bench, prepared, in literature as in life, to handle and judge any situation. That is why the reader gets teased so frankly.'

clever justifications for his behaviour), and that is all there is to it.

I have already tried to show, through a detailed analysis of Blifil's speech of excuse, why this answer won't do. Blifil's own words, given the context in which they are uttered, systematically undercut his claim to be a romantically impulsive servant of either God or Liberty: the casuistical precision with which the speech is put together makes us doubt its genuineness as the product of childish moral impetuosity from the beginning, and the barbed references to Tommy's fate and to Tom's causal implication in it which come at the end resolve the issue with complete finality: this is not the voice of an overly bookish but fundamentally well-meaning child; it is the voice of a confident and malicious little boy whose cunning is overreaching itself.

Coleridge, if anything, understates his case. To say 'we *feel* him to be so' suggests that our conviction that he is so is a mere intuition for which no rational justification can be given. I don't think moral perception is ever as diaphanous as that, whatever gutter-Romanticism and the efforts of philosophers to prove the essential irrationality of moral judgement may have conditioned us to think. Certainly it is not so in this case. We can, as we have seen, defend the judgement that Blifil is a villain by detailed reference to what he says and the context in which he says it, and so far as I can see the case which Blifil thus unwittingly makes against himself is an entirely conclusive one. Hence, if knowledge is, as Professor Ayer[23] assures us, belief for which sound reasons can be given, we have (Fielding gives us, that is) knowledge of Blifil's character. Moreover *pace* Kermode, the reader needs no community of moral sentiment with Fielding or Western in order to understand the force of the reasons for thinking Blifil a villain. He does not have to be *un homme moyen sensuel*, or a 'decent chap', or a 'genuinely good humoured, high spirited, humane, orthodox gentleman of the eighteenth century'. He needs a moderate level of skill at weighing and sifting the kind of evidence which enables us to judge character in everyday life (we do this, it is important to remember, on the basis of what people say and do over long periods of time and in many contexts, not on the basis of

[23] A. J. Ayer, *The Problem of Knowledge*, Penguin, Chapter 1.

telepathic awareness of their inner thoughts), but the exercise of this sort of skill is not, or need not be, dependent upon the moral outlook or sympathies of the man who exercises it: it *can* be quite neutral with respect to moral *partis pris*, though of course the exercise of it may be affected, on occasion, by moral predilections. I may overlook, or mistake for honest political enthusiasm, behaviour which, if a political opponent exhibited it, I should recognise immediately as a combination of ambition, spleen and malice. But that does not mean that it is impossible to have conclusive grounds, derived from observation of a man's discourse and behaviour, for attributing such motives to him (the reasons for which Blifil's claim to be considered impulsively generous fall to the ground afford a case in point); it just means that my judgement is clouded by party prejudice.

III

We know what Blifil *is* because Blifil gives himself away. But may that not merely be because Blifil at that point in the story is so young, and as yet relatively unpractised in deceit? If I am right, and the case to be made from Blifil's words against his sincerity is conclusive, then this possibility would not matter from the point of view of how Fielding's method works in this one example. But it would argue nonetheless a serious defect in Fielding's method construed as a *general* technique for the delineation of the relationship of underlying character to surface conduct. If the objection stands, that is, Fielding's technique will work only for characters who can be plausibly supposed to be incapable of giving a more accomplished imitation of virtue than Blifil's. And since few characters in novels, Fielding's included, are vicious twelve-year-old children, this severely limits the applicability of the method.

This objection, which I think strikes one at first sight as sound and persuasive, seems to me to be based on a quite interesting and important error about the connection between motives and the behaviour which, truly or falsely, manifests them. The error is that of forgetting that when a man wants to feign, through his behaviour, motives which he does not really possess, he is restricted in the means he may adopt to accomplish this end by the requirement that he set about it in a way which will satisfy his audience that he is *by their standards and from their point of view* virtuous, and in addition by the need to continue pursuing his real goals. It is not at all clear that, in practice, the best way to give people the impression that B is one's goal is to behave exactly as somebody would behave if he sincerely wanted to achieve B and was oblivious to, or cared nothing for, any other consideration. In fact it seems pretty obvious that it is not; and it is this very lesson which, as it happens, the plot of *Tom Jones* is largely designed to enforce. *Tom Jones* abounds with examples of innocence misunderstood. Jenny Jones' innocent pride in her Latin is taken by Partridge's virago of a wife as evidence of a secret affair with Partridge. Tom's delight at Allworthy's recovery is taken for a time, by a man of no less sound moral intelligence than Allworthy himself, as drunken disregard for his benefactor's illness. Examples multiply: they are part of that running demonstration of the necessity of prudence to the practice of goodness which has often been re-marked in the book, but which Fielding's Richardsonian critics disregarded in their anxiety to prove the book immoral. But the point has implications for the technique of the novel as well. If prudence is needful to the good man it is equally needful to the dissimulating villain.

His prudence, however, is a matter of sound public relations, and this involves suiting the evidence which he chooses to give of virtuous goals to the audience for which it is intended. Had Blifil chosen to give a perfect imitation of an impulsively generous but wetly thoughtless child, tearfully apologising to Sophia and joining her in doleful howls at the demise of Tommy, the response of Thwackum and Square, neither of them men to tolerate romantic mawkishness (though Square would no doubt deem it inconsistent with rational magnanimity and Thwackum with Christian fortitude), can easily be imagined. Blifil's status as a favoured pupil might have spared him the thrashing which would have been Tom's lot in similar circumstances, but he would still have lapsed regrettably in their eyes into behaviour more characteristic of the scoundrel Tom, even though the latter would no doubt have taken some of the blame for bad influence. Mere prudence would declare this too high a price to pay for satisfaction of a casual malicious impulse: hence Blifil must, for practical purposes, pitch his sights as a dissimulator lower than theoretical perfection, even in public.

The ironic contrast between the failure of innocence and simplicity to meet with any credence in the world, and the success of pious fraud, is a constant theme of *Tom Jones* (the deliberate theatrical implausibility of the happy ending drives it home: in real life, we are to understand, Blifil and not Tom would have ended as master of Paradise Hall and of Sophia). But the practical exigencies of dissimulation also afford Fielding a tool for the dissection of character. Dissimulation in practice involves more than a simple contrast between real goals and simulated goals. Deceit about goals necessarily commits those who practise it to a third goal, over and above their real, or primary, goals (in Blifil's case, spite) and the goals they are trying to simulate (in Blifil's case, libertarian compassion); namely, the goal of presenting their behaviour in the best possible light to the people they actually have to deal with. The deceitful man must make plausibility his first, although not his primary, goal.

It is this last proviso which is the important one. We have been talking so far – or rather our hypothetical critic has been talking – as if the claim that we can ascribe goals to people on the basis of their observed behaviour entailed the claim that goals are associated with standard behavioural stereotypes (The Conduct of the Avaricious Man, The Conduct of the Benevolent Man, etc.) and that it is enough to assume one of these stereotypes to be recognised anywhere, by anybody, as somebody who possesses the corresponding goal. This is of course absurd. Pretending to be impulsively generous when I am not, or avaricious when I am not, involves making all sorts of assumptions about the character and viewpoint of the person to whom I am putting up the pretence; and of course this brings into play my own character, assumptions and viewpoint: in the way I judge or estimate others I reveal myself.

Pretence is always, then, pretence relative to the person for whose benefit I am putting up the pretence, and when it succeeds its success is similarly relative. Pretence, when it works, does not work *tout court*: it works *on somebody*.

And hence all its machinations may stand revealed from a third viewpoint, from which both the character of the person who could be fooled by such a pretence, and the character of the pretender, as shown by the estimate he has evidently formed of the man confronting him, may be evident. In short, from a third point of view the falsity of the pretence shows in inconsistencies between the goals pretended to and the machinery of the pretence itself, machinery which is *necessarily* only invisible from the point of view of the person or persons against whom the successful masquerade is directed.

The revelation of character in Fielding (the securing of the contrast which Coleridge noticed between what a character *does* and what he *is*) generally works through this device of shifting viewpoints rotating, as it were, the angle of vision; I think it is clear that this is what is going on in the episode of the caged bird. Blifil, Thwackum and Square are locked in the smug, blind complicity of deceiver and deceived. The nature of the deceit is invisible to Thwackum and Square and I think – I shall have more to say about this later – that it is in part invisible to Blifil. But from the reader's point of view it is palpable. And what reveals the likely nature of Blifil's motives in freeing the bird is precisely that the spirit and mechanisms of the speech which Blifil must make in order to secure his credit with the tutors are, when seen from the point of view occupied by the reader, blankly and systematically at odds with the character which Blifil wishes to assume and which from the tutors' point of view he has succeeded in assuming.

Because the grand design of *Tom Jones*, in the service of which Fielding deploys this technique, is a moral design, Fielding critics seem perennially tempted to confuse the technique itself with moralising; in other words, to read the novel as a sermon with illustrations. No doubt this is why people often find Fielding's characters wooden: this way of reading depends on systematic failure to grasp what gives them life. Robert Alter, a recent defender of Fielding, in a book which contains much that is worth reading, nonetheless expresses the conventional view:

> The detailed psychological realisation of character has been assumed to be so basic to the novel that I think it is worth considering how Fielding manages to get along without it. There are times, to be sure, when his balanced judgement

of characters comes to the brink of psychological analysis; what is to be learned, however, from such moments is not that Fielding is an unfulfilled psychologist but rather that generalised moral assessment can be an effective novelistic substitute for detailed psychological rendering.[24]

I hope I have already said enough to make clear the distinction between the revelation of character by playing off one viewpoint against another, and mere moralising. But it may help to see that the technique is not peculiar to Fielding, nor intrinsically bound up with his moral position; although it connects him more with modern fiction than with the main stream of the eighteenth- and nineteenth-century novel. Here it is again, deployed this time without irony and without forming part of a grand moral design, in the encounter between Marcel and the snobbish M. Legrandin in *Swann's Way*:

> I summoned up all my courage and said to him: 'Tell me, sir, do you, by any chance, know the lady – the ladies of Guermantes?' and I felt glad because, in pronouncing the name, I had secured a sort of power over it, by the mere act of drawing it up out of my dreams and giving it an objective existence in the world of spoken things.
>
> But at the sound of the word Guermantes, I saw in the middle of each of our friend's blue eyes a little brown dimple appear, as though they had been stabbed by some invisible pin-point, while the rest of his pupils, reacting from the shock, received and secreted the azure overflow. His fringed eyelids darkened and drooped. His mouth, which had been stiffened and seared with bitter lines, was the first to recover, and smiled, while his eyes still seemed full of pain,

[24] Robert Alter, *Fielding and the Nature of the Novel*, Harvard University Press, 1968, p. 69. I am in a way being unfair to Alter here; a few pages later he notices that 'the closely related activity of irony also has the effect at times of making the characters more lifelike and complex', and that 'irony as Fielding uses it is more than a means of limited access to character'. My point is, however, that we shall never get clear about *how* Fielding's irony gives him 'access to character' if we cannot say clearly what distinguishes the revelation of character through irony from mere *moralising about* characters. That Alter is happy with the phrase 'generalised moral evaluation' shows that he is, to say the least, not altogether clear about the problem, or about the real force of the implicit criticism of Fielding which hangs upon it.

like the eyes of a good-looking martyr whose body bristles with arrows.

'No, I do not know them,' he said, but instead of uttering so simple a piece of information, a reply in which there was so little that would astonish me, in the natural and conventional tone that would have befitted it, he recited it with a separate stress on each word, leaning forward, bowing his head, with at once the vehemence which a man gives, so as to be believed, to a highly improbable statement (as though the fact that he did not know the Guermantes could be due only to some strange accident of fortune) and with the emphasis of a man who, finding himself unable to keep silent about what is to him a painful situation, chooses to proclaim it aloud, so as to convince his hearers that the confession he is making is one that causes him no embarrassment, but is easy, agreeable, spontaneous, that the situation in question, in this case the absence of relations with the Guermantes family, might very well have been not forced upon, but actually designed by Legrandin himself, might arise from some family tradition, some moral principle or mystical vow which expressly forbade his seeking their society.

'No,' he resumed, explaining by his words the tone in which they were uttered. 'No, I do not know them; I have never wished to know them; I have always made a point of preserving complete independence; at heart, as you know, I am a bit of a Radical. People are always coming to me about it, telling me I am mistaken in not going to Guermantes, that I make myself seem ill-bred, uncivilised, an old bear. But that's not the sort of reputation that can frighten me; it's too true! In my heart of hearts I care for nothing in the world now but a few churches, books – two or three, pictures – rather more perhaps, and the light of the moon when the fresh breeze of youth wafts to my nostrils the scent of gardens whose flowers my old eyes are not sharp enough, now, to distinguish.'[25]

Like Blifil, Legrandin goes on far too long, and in altogether the wrong tone of voice. He is not really addressing the boy in

[25] Marcel Proust, *Swann's Way*, Scott Moncrieff translation, Chatto and Windus, illustrated edition, 1957, pp. 173–4.

front of him, who finds it wholly unsurprising that Legrandin should not be on visiting terms with a great lady whom he, Marcel, regards as an almost supernatural being. It is Legrandin himself who (as Proust says, like a martyr in a picture who casts his wronged reproachful gaze up to heaven as the unmerited arrows bristle in his flesh) feels the fact that he does not know the Guermantes as a scandalous anomaly, demanding explanation. And the explanations: that he is a bear, a Jacobin at heart, a man who likes to retain his independence, an elderly epicurean retired, having renounced courts and Duchesses, to the contemplation of beauty and the transience of youth (explanations too numerous, too disparate and at best only sketchily congruent with one another), tumble out of him.

Proust's point, however, is not that any of these explanations is particularly implausible in itself. Rather it is that the *giving* of the explanations is itself inconsistent with the claim to be a Jacobin at heart, or an elderly epicurean who has renounced the world, because a person of any of these kinds would, precisely, not be giving explanations at this point: the *tête de Jacobin*, because he would shudder away from the very thought of any such demeaning babble, the more so the more he actually felt the weight of the Guermantes' indifference; the epicurean sage because the Guermantes' acquaintance genuinely would not matter to him, and so on.

Later Proust says:

> Certainly that is not to say that M. Legrandin was not sincere when he inveighed against snobs. He could not know, at least of himself, that he was one, since we can be acquainted only with the passions of others, and whatever knowledge we come to have of our own can only have been acquired from them. (My translation.)[26]

This is, if you like, merely *telling* us about Legrandin: that he is a snob and doesn't know it. We have not seen Legrandin's snobbery manifest itself in the way Kermode seems to require; through an exemplary act causally connected up with a realistically depicted inner life. And yet we feel that

[26] Marcel Proust, *Du Coté de chez Swann*, Gallimard 1954, *Le Livre de Poche* p. 155.

Legrandin has revealed himself to us, and that Proust is not telling us about him, but merely commenting on features of his character which are already and independently apparent to the reader. We have the Coleridgean sense that we know what Legrandin *is*. And we get it, I think, through exactly the same mechanism of shifting between concordant and opposed viewpoints as operates in the case of Blifil and the bird, and in general throughout *Tom Jones*. Legrandin is speaking to an imaginary (or better, assumed) interlocutor who, like himself, sees failure to be on visiting terms with the Guermantes as a sad, shocking and extraordinary state of affairs, needing explanation. Legrandin's explanations might, indeed, succeed if they fell upon the ears of such an interlocutor. But instead they are addressed to the alien viewpoint of the boy Marcel, a snob of a very different sort who, because he feels quasi-religious veneration for the Guermantes, sees nothing odd in anyone's not knowing them. The mere existence of this viewpoint breaks the spell in which the reader would be held if he were constrained to think of the absence of relations with the Guermantes as something requiring explanation (if that were a suggested but unexamined premise of the novel, for example), and under which he might well accept that Legrandin really is a Jacobin or an epicurean despiser of the world. From Marcel's viewpoint the fact that Legrandin's speech is implicitly directed to someone who is assumed to hold it extraordinary not to know the Guermantes *stands out*; this throws into relief the incongruity of the explanations offered with the fact that explanations are *being* offered; and this makes it clear that the point of view to which the speech is addressed is indeed Legrandin's own.

The justice of Proust's anti-Cartesian remark that we know our own passions derivatively from what we know of other people's is evident from this. Legrandin might indeed come to know himself as a snob if he could only 'hear himself talk'. But hearing himself talk here means listening to how his talk sounds from Marcel's point of view. Similarly Blifil might realise that something was going wrong with his speech if, for example, he caught sight, in mid-stride, of a sardonic smile on the lips of one of the company. But he could only know *what* was going wrong by looking at the speech from the bystander's point of view. Then he would know what was wrong with the speech and what the sardonic smile meant, but to arrive at this knowledge he would have to come to understand the bystander. Introspection, the examination of his own consciousness, could not reveal to him the meaning of the bystander's smile, and so it could not reveal to him the nature of his own heart. And if knowledge of Blifil's consciousness could not, in these respects, reveal him to himself, it is hard to see how, in these respects, it could reveal him to us; to Fielding's readers.

We seem driven, in short, to conclude that certain kinds of knowledge of a man's inwardness, of what he is, are easier to convey through the ironic juxtaposition of viewpoints than through the creation of an illusion of direct knowledge of a character's stream of consciousness. Descartes was wrong to think that my knowledge of my own mind is perfect, and the primary source of all my knowledge. This is the drift, or part of the drift, of Wittgenstein's remark to the effect that even if God knew the contents of my mind he would still not know what I was thinking. The question 'What am I just now thinking?', let alone the question, 'What am I?' is never fully settled, or settleable, by introspection.

We can now look back at Empson's remark, quoted earlier, on Fielding as a delineator of character.

I take it he refused to believe that the 'inside' of a person's mind, as given by Richardson in a letter, perhaps, is much use for telling you the real source of his motives. You learn that from what he does, and therefore a novelist ought to devise an illustrative plot.

With the first sentence of this I fully agree. But I don't think that it is the 'illustrative' plot which chiefly serves to reveal character in *Tom Jones*. For Fielding the contrast between a man's real nature and the surface he presents to the world cannot be identified either with the contrast between inner consciousness and behaviour or with the contrast between what he says and what he does (although certainly the second identification, which I take to be Empson's, comes closer than the first to being correct). Rather it is the contrast between what an interlocutor, looking at what a character says and does from a particular viewpoint, might make of him, and what a second interlocutor or a spectator, able to survey both from a second viewpoint, might make of the commerce between them. Fielding's concept of character, in short, is founded in the notion of the coherence of a man's speech and action when seen from different viewpoints; and further, in the nation that only truth and simplicity can survive, without lapsing into incoherence of the sort we have been examining, the scrutiny it must undergo as the planes and mirrors of transposed points of view turn and shift about it.

IV

Fielding is everywhere boisterously present in *Tom Jones*: Richardson is scrupulously absent from *Pamela*.[27] If what we have just said is correct, there are good reasons for Fielding's constant authorial presence. If we are to read the book as Fielding intended us to read it we must be constantly aware of the possibility of changing the viewpoint from which we perceive any incident in it. It is essential to this method that no viewpoint should be regarded as 'privileged'; especially not the reader's. We have already given a minor example of this in the case of Western's contributions to the casuistical debate which follows the bird episode. Western is plainly a booby squire: but is he, or is that all he is? The reader cannot be allowed to repose in place upon his own judgement: he must be forced out of it constantly, made to distrust the viewpoint he is most naturally disposed to fall into, otherwise the method of ironically playing off one point of view, one vision of what is going on in a particular episode, against another cannot work on him. It is thus peculiarly unfair to Fielding, and peculiarly dense, to suggest that his method as a novelist works only because of a covert complicity between author and reader: it is precisely such a complicity which Fielding must subvert if his method is to work

[27] "The formal difference between Richardson and Fielding is absolutely radical; a matter of their whole way of seeing, creating and ordering, long before there is any question of their moral or social attitudes. In Richardson 'the author' disappears; in Fielding he is omnipresent and all-important . . . Fielding prevents us from getting involved (where Richardson ensures that we are); he will use mock-heroic, or an elaborate and heightened rhetoric, to hold us at arms length, keep us looking from the outside, and make us take the essential point of the scene within the whole pattern." Mark Kincaid-Weekes, *Samuel Richardson*, Methuen, 1973, pp. 468–9.

at all. And so he works ceaselessly to subvert it, endlessly stopping the film so that he can walk at leisure round his characters thus frozen in the midst of their activity, pointing out, or more often indicating by irony or tone of voice, the multifarious significances of the situation in which they find themselves. The object of these interruptions is not anxiously to enforce the 'right' moral reactions upon the reader, but to force him continually to recognise that what he is confronted by is not reality but a fiction.[28]

Kermode, and many other critics as well, have construed the novel of psychological realism as one in which the author 'lets events talk'. This is why Kermode admires Richardson as one who chose 'to draw his breath in pain and tell the story'. I have my doubts about the extent and purity of the category of psychologically realist fiction which this thumbnail sketch delineates, but no doubt this doesn't matter much: Kermode's point is that this is how the novel works at its best, and that it is when it is most like this that it is most worthy of serious attention.

To the extent to which a novel works in this way, it must strive to create in the reader the sense that he is becoming acquainted with real people and real events: hence the necessary self-effacement of the author. The criterion of 'reality' in the required sense is, as Kermode rightly suggests, *causal* coherence. The actions of the characters must admit of plausible causal explanation in terms of their states of mind, and vice versa. The questions before the reader are thus characteristically 'Why does he do that?' and correlatively 'What does this action reveal about him?'; 'Why does Pamela order the coach turned back?', 'What leads Henchard to attempt to defeat Farfrae in corn dealing?', 'What evidence have we for thinking that Elinor is not cold hearted towards Edward Ferrars?', and so on.

There is no reason why interest in the causal coherence of action and character should not coexist in the same novel with interest in the way in which the significance, the moral credentials, the tone of voice, of discourse changes as we construe it from different points of view. It is part of Jane Austen's great-

[28] Readers of Gabriel Josipovici's *The World and The Book* will recognise the influence of his thought upon mine here.

46

ness that both techniques cohabit inextricably in her novels. We know that Elinor is not cold hearted towards Edward Ferrars because the tone of heat and fluster in which she leaps to his defence is not like her.[29] But we know it also because we see how stilted and chilly her defence appears from Marianne's viewpoint, turning as it does upon the offensive word 'esteem' – and because we know enough already about the silliness of Marianne's viewpoint for this to act as a check upon any hasty tendency the reader might feel to view the speech in the same light himself, and sends him back a little shamefacedly to reconsider his first impressions of what Elinor has said (reflecting, for example, that 'esteem' is really a perfectly sensible and appropriate word, and that Marianne's contempt for it expresses a fashionable but in her case almost wholly automatic romanticism).

But nevertheless the two techniques are intrinsically inimical to one another, and it takes genius to get them to work in tandem. Psychological realism rests on the assumption that the reader's viewpoint is valid, in the sense that from it he can perceive all that he needs to perceive in order to arrive at a proper grasp of the causal interconnections of action and inner-life in the novel. This privileged viewpoint is, of course, merely the other side of the coin of authorial omniscience: the reader knows 'the facts', and knows that they are all relevant facts, and all the facts that *are* relevant, because they are the facts the author has chosen to lay before him. Hence, once having constructed his fiction the author can, as it were, steal away, leaving the reader to confront the events of the book just as he would a slice of real life, only, of course, with a cast-iron certainty of the adequacy of the vision of reality afforded him by his point of view *qua* reader which is sadly lacking in *real* real life. Authorial presence is necessarily a nuisance, if this is the kind of novel you are writing: it gets between the reader and 'the facts' which are to be allowed to 'speak for themselves', and hence authorial presence in such a novel is *prima facie* a defect: it shows that the author has not done his work properly: has not arranged his fictional 'facts' so that they *can* speak for themselves. Like Newton's God he must intrude to adjust the motions of an imperfect creation which cannot run smoothly by itself. That is

[29] Jane Austen, *Sense and Sensibility*, Chapter IV.

47

the substance and the rationale of Kermode's criticisms of Fielding.

But, on the other hand, authorial absence is equally inimical to Fielding's chosen technique. It is essential to that technique that the reader should not enjoy the luxury of a viewpoint guaranteed in advance to be one from which the truth about the characters can be discovered. For the point implicit in Fielding's technique of ironically juxtaposing and contrasting points of view,[30] of exposing actions simultaneously to being morally and psychologically construed from more than one direction; is that no *one* viewpoint is ever 'guaranteed'; ever wholly adequate as a basis from which to grasp the nature of human reality. The point is the one Proust makes explicit: that in learning whatever I manage to learn about character, whether others' or my own, I must transcend the point of view I most comfortably occupy, projecting myself into others by an effort of imagination. Hence the gusto with which Fielding continually teases the reader and mocks his preconceptions: he must be kept off balance so that, missing his footing in one viewpoint he will regain it momentarily in another and so learn that perpetual motion of the imagination from which dispassionate moral judgement and understanding of others both grow: in real life, if not in books.

Of course, this technique *is* hostile to psychological realism. Authorial presence *does* prevent the building of an illusion of reality: of the facts speaking for themselves. And an interest in the coherence or incoherence of the 'public' surface of a man's discourse and action as we ironically vary the imaginative viewpoint from which we regard it does in Fielding almost wholly drive out any interest in the causal coherence of action and inner life, as in Jane Austen it does not (Jane Austen's authorial presence is far subtler and less intrusive than Fielding's and her irony less bludgeoning, though as accurate: but then her aims are different). The Johnsonian tradition is thus, in a sense, quite correct so far as the truth of the observations which they construe as criticisms of Fielding goes. My point is simply that these observations are not *criticisms*. What adverse critics construe as

[30] Empson, in the paper quoted earlier, calls this 'double irony'. I think, though I am not altogether sure, that he and I are talking about the same thing.

incompetence in Fielding's treatment of character is only incompetence from the point of view of a theory of the novel, and a theory of the nature of knowledge of character, which happen not to apply to Fielding's novels. Fielding, just as well as Richardson, can paint the inwardness of a man's character. Only it is not 'inwardness' in the same sense; not the Cartesian 'inwardness' of consciousness; of the 'private', interior, mental world, as opposed to the public world of discourse and behaviour. Fielding's distinction between a man's real and his apparent nature is drawn *within* the public world.

V

Experience has taught me to expect that English philosophers and critics alike will object to the above arguments on the ground that they seem to imply that there is no such thing as reality at all. If all my knowledge, of myself as of others, is relative to the viewpoint from which I construe my experience and if any viewpoint can always be exchanged for another, from which things may appear different, where is there any firm footing? How can I really know anything? Don't such arguments lead, not to a new theory of the novel, but merely to a sterile cognitive nihilism?

To forestall these objections, therefore, I had better emphasise that what I am saying is not that no viewpoint reveals *anything* about reality, but (1) that no viewpoint reveals *everything* about reality, and (2) that there are some kinds of knowledge, including some kinds of self-knowledge, that can only be acquired by looking at things from two or more points of view at once.

Fielding really does, that is, afford the reader the means of coming to *know* that Blifil is a scoundrel; Proust's Legrandin is revealed as *in reality* a snob; *pace*, even, whatever Legrandin's own introspection might tell him: at such points the novel of publicity (publicity in the philosophical sense that is) really does touch bottom in indubitable facts, even though (it would be more accurate to say because) it dispenses with the technique of offering the reader a privileged position of temporary omniscience. But the kind of knowledge the reader acquires in this way can only be acquired if the reader is willing to think about what he is reading in a certain special way; to project himself imaginatively into several viewpoints, rather than to relapse into passivity in the assurance that he is being conducted by an infallible guide (this is not to say that major realist novels require no thought of their readers: they require thought of a different kind). This indeed has as its implication that the reader's viewpoint is not privileged; but that in turn does *not* mean that he is plunged into a world in which he can be sure of grasping *nothing* that is going on in the novel.

Fielding at one point (Book III, Chapter 5) serves notice quite explicitly upon the reader that this is his situation:

> the reader is greatly mistaken, if he conceives that Thwackum appeared to Allworthy in the same light as he doth to him in this history; and he is as much deceived, if he imagines that the most intimate acquaintance which he himself could have had with that divine, would have informed him of those things which we by our inspiration are enabled to discover. Of readers who, from such conceits as these, condemn the wisdom and penetration of Mr. Allworthy, I shall not scruple to say, that they make a very bad and ungrateful use of that knowledge which we have communicated to them.

3
RECONSTITUTIVE IRONY

I

There is also, of course, a discursive, buttonholing Fielding who tells us at length about his characters and their situation. In that way he creates an elaborate moral, social and psychological context for a series of moral vignettes like the bird episode. What is easily missed is that the vignettes are not themselves just further doses of descriptive assertion on the part of the author. Once launched into them the characters lead independent lives, though the mechanism by which they do so is the one described in the last chapter, and not that of psychological realism. The vignettes are not, therefore, puppet shows: they offer *confirmation*, and not merely amplification, of Fielding's judgements upon his characters. They give the alert reader *the materials he needs to form his own judgement* about the characters.

Fielding was aware that *Tom Jones* has this structure, and makes a distinction between incident and description which in places becomes entirely explicit. Thus Fielding introduces the two boys in a passage of heavily sarcastic description.

> The vices of this young man were, moreover, heightened by the disadvantageous light in which they appeared when opposed to the virtues of Master Blifil, his companion; a youth of so different a cast from little Jones, that not only the family but all the neighbourhood resounded his praises.[31] He

[31] The humour of this lies, of course, in Fielding's dismal but acute estimate of the average level of generosity, fair-mindedness and common veracity, abroad in an English village or small town. Local rumour and moralising gossip in *Tom Jones* invariably gets everything back to front, as witness, for example, its recorded judgements of Partridge, Black George or Jenny Jones, and its weathercock vacillations of opinion over the various fates of Tom himself. For this aspect of Fielding's mind it is worth looking also at the moving passage in the *Voyage to Lisbon* in which he recounts the carrying of his hideous, dropsical carcase aboard ship to the tune of resounding jeers and catcalls from the assembled porters and shipmen. Fielding had, after all, some reason to feel pessimistic about the prevalence of common humanity. That his pessimism was not absolute can be seen, for example, in his treatment of the long-suffering lieutenant of dragoons who takes Tom's part against Ensign Northerton.

was, indeed, a lad of remarkable disposition: sober, discreet, and pious beyond his age; qualities which gained him the love of every one who knew him: while Tom Jones was universally disliked; and many expressed their wonder that Mr. Allworthy would suffer such a lad to be educated with his nephew, lest the morals of the latter should be corrupted by his example.

But he follows this at once with an admission of the relative impotence of authorial assertion and gets on at once to the main business of submitting the matter to the judgement of the reader.

An incident which happened about this time will set the characters of the two lads more firmly before the discerning reader than is in the power of the longest dissertation.

The incident in question is the episode of Tom's ill-advised foray on to Western's land in the company of Black George, which gives rise to much pointed conversation revelatory of character through the same mechanisms as those operating in the caged bird episode.

Of course, if you think that 'judging a man's character' is no more than deciding, on the basis of whatever subjective moral preferences you yourself happen to subscribe to, whether you like or dislike the way he carries on, this is a distinction without a difference. But then, if moral judgement is as arbitrary and subjective as this, more collapses than my case in favour of Fielding. The claim of the novel in general to be a serious art form collapses as well; for if the judgement of moral character comes in the end merely to subjective preference, the novel can be no more than, at most, a useful instrument for inculcating or reinforcing the moral prejudices of readers.[32] But in fact, as I

[32] Johnson, who believed in the novel as an instrument of moral didacticism, might, oddly enough, not have been too unhappy with this consequence; despite his praise of Richardson for his skill in depicting the inner life of consciousness, which seems to link him to later, anti-didactic, versions of realism. It should not be forgotten that Fielding's critics objected to his claim to transcribe characters from nature on the grounds that one ought to use moral criteria in deciding which aspects of nature to transcribe (this is part of the force of the 'lowness' charge. See The Rambler, No. 4, for example, and Fielding's preface to Book VII of Tom Jones).

have tried to show in my analysis of the caged bird episode, moral judgement is nothing like as arbitrary or subjective as the above view suggests.

To say this, of course, is merely to say that words like 'generous', 'malicious', 'friendship', 'envy', and so on, have definite meanings.[33] I cannot apply them arbitrarily or at will, if I am to speak intelligible English; which is in turn to say no more than what is, after all, trivially true; that a word whose application depends solely on the whim of the speaker, like the word 'runcible' in Lewis Carroll's verse, is precisely not a real word at all, but a nonsense epithet.[34]

An obvious way of getting people to recollect the full weight and force of a word is to use it in a way which weakens and vitiates its force. It doesn't always work, of course: at the moment, for example, many people seem quite happy to use 'refute' as if it had the same force as 'deny'. If the tendency prevails, and 'refute' becomes a synonym for 'deny', English will have suffered a slight and absolute impoverishment. It will still be possible to say that someone has refuted an argument, as distinct from merely having denied its conclusion, but only by means of a circumlocution. There will be no *word* for the concept of refutation, and so it will become a little more 'academic' and *recherché*; a little less readily available to ordinary speakers of the language. And this will make the distinction between denial and refutation a little harder to recollect and to bear in mind.

But of course the misuse of words can work both ways. While some sense of its full meaning survives, the misuse of a word can still cause discomfort; the sense that something is missing: and when this is sufficiently acute it can rouse us into an active effort to discover *what* is missing; to try to recollect and to

[33] Those who are familiar with recent philosophical writing on ethics will want to ask whether what I have in mind is 'factual' or 'descriptive' meaning or 'emotive' meaning. The answer is, neither. I think the conventional positivist dichotomy between factual and emotive meaning is a false dichotomy, for reasons which will become clear as the book progresses.

[34] This is a trivial statement, of course, but one which, like some trivial propositions in mathematics, is rich in consequences. I have tried to draw out some of these in my books *Meaning and Structure*, Harper & Row, N.Y., 1972; *Form and Content*, Blackwell, Oxford, 1974; and *Philosophy of Language*, Macmillan.

formulate more explicitly the distinctions which loose talk is slurring and burying.[35]

There is a case for a special term here. I want to speak of *logical parody*: the construction of parodic or pastiche examples of the use of a word which force us to recollect how the word should really be used if it is to bear its full weight.

The construction of logical parodies is an essentially philosophical enterprise. Wittgenstein's later writings are full of examples of the technique: it is one of the chief sorts of thing he has in mind, I think, when he says that the task of philosophy is to 'assemble reminders' of the way our ordinary conceptual scheme works. It is a technique which favours certain sorts of philosophical enterprise and conclusion over others. To be precise, it is an *anti-reductionist* technique. A philosophical theory is reductionist in character when it invites us to dispense with certain conceptual distinctions which we ordinarily make, on the grounds that, viewed from a more fundamental point of view (in some sense of 'more fundamental' which it is of course the job of the reductionist philosopher in question to make clear to his readers) they are baseless. Berkeley, for example, is advancing a reductionist thesis when he tries to show that the distinction between physical objects (construed as *extra-mental* entities) and the experiences we have of physical objects is one which cannot, in the end, be drawn because it implicitly contains a contradiction (the exact nature of the contradiction is matter of dispute, but it is something like supposing that perceptions could exist unperceived). Likewise, when Hobbes, defining pity in his analysis of the passions in Chapter 6 of Part I of *Leviathan*, says:

[35] Glenn W. Hatfield, in *Henry Fielding and the Language of Irony*, University of Chicago Press, 1968, p. 165, describes the technique with admirable clarity: 'The very words which must carry the heaviest thematic freight are systematically turned inside out, not in order to proclaim cynically, in the manner of Mandeville, that emptiness is their natural condition, nor to measure, in the manner of Swift, the impassable distance between the reality and the ideal, but to create a vacuum of meaning which cries out to be filled. Irony . . . thus becomes a kind of negative test of truth. For only when the word is united with its 'proper idea', only, that is, when a meaning is provided that fulfils the word's implicit promise and accounts for its dignity of connotation, will the ironic alarm fail to sound.'

> *Grief,* for the calamity of another, is PITY; and ariseth
> from the imagination that the like calamity may befall him-
> self; and therefore is called also COMPASSION, and in the
> phrase of this present time a FELLOW-FEELING . . .

he is in effect defining the word 'pity' out of the English
language. For, if he is right, he is reducing the concept of pity
to the concept of pain felt for another man's distress, arising
from the thought that the same distress might overtake me. If
this reduction succeeds it follows that we can say everything
that people ordinarily manage to say in availing themselves of
the word 'pity', provided only that we can still avail ourselves
of the words 'pain' (or 'grief') and 'fear'. If we have those, we
don't need 'pity'. For (to put exactly the same point as a point
about reality rather than a point about language) pity is just a
variety of pain, or grief; and not an emotion existing in its own
right, separate and distinct from pain or grief.

A reductionist argument has two components, which are
seldom clearly separated from one another. On the one hand
there is an attempt to formulate the meaning of a word, together
with the claim that this is the only sense the word will 'really'
bear. And then, on the other hand there must be an argument
of some sort to supply this later claim with teeth, or to put it
another way, to give a sense to the crucial adverb 'really'.
Countering a reductionist argument similarly involves two
separate but seldom distinguished strands of argument. On the
one hand the anti-reductionist must show that we cannot dispense with the conceptual distinctions which the reductionist
wishes to do away with: that there *appear*, at least, to be truths
about the world which we cannot utter unless we dispose, for
example, of the word, and the concept, pity; and which we
should not be able to utter if we disposed only of the concepts
of pain and fear. And on the other hand he must show *why* this
is so: he must give a positive account of the meaning of, say,
'pity' which shows not only *that* but *why* we cannot dispense
with the word, and hence why the thing itself cannot be treated
as a variant of pain, or fear, or any other passion.

Fielding – and this is one source of the philosophical subtlety
which I find in him – attempts both these anti-reductive tasks
for the conceptual vocabulary of morals: for 'generosity', 'hate',

'friendship', 'courage', 'prudence', and the rest of our catalogue of subordinate moral concepts; and for that concept which Plato and platonising modern philosophers like G. E. Moore place at their head, as the primary concept which gives meaning to all the rest: 'good'. The first task, that of reminding the reader of how moral concepts function and of how moral distinctions are made in everyday life; of forcing him to recollect in detail the full weight and force of these concepts in the face of pressures to thin and weaken them (pressures coming on the one hand from ordinary moral self-deception and on the other from reductionist philosophy of one sort and another), is performed by the whole fabric of the novel, taken as a fabric of reconstitutive irony. The second, more theoretical task, of displaying the articulations of these multifarious insights, of showing that joint derivation from a single conceptual root, is performed by Fielding's much-despised theory of the Good Heart. Taken together, the fabric of irony which is the novel itself, and the theory of the Good Heart form, as I shall try to show, an impressive theoretical structure. It is the presence of this structure, I think, which accounts for Empson's sense that the novel is 'proving a case', that it 'builds up like Euclid'.

And yet 'theoretical structure' is the wrong phrase. It suggests that *Tom Jones* is merely an illustrated argument: that the structure of sound theory which the book contains could be extracted like the backbone of a herring, to be stated and defended with perfect adequacy on its own terms as a piece of philosophy. To suppose this would be to neglect everything that we have just been saying, in this and the previous chapter, about Fielding's technique. The *mode* of argument by which Fielding attacks reductionist accounts of morality belongs essentially to literature and not to philosophy, even though it has the effects of (rather good) philosophical argument. Fielding does not, in other words, present the reader with an abstractly formulated thesis illustrated by bare and schematic 'examples'. He draws him, as spectator and judge, into a complex imagined world in which he must actually exercise moral judgement in circumstances *which force him to reflect upon what he is doing in making such judgements,* and upon the difference between making such judgements in a full consciousness of what the words employed in them really mean, and making them with the kind of inattention to meaning which can spring equally from vulgar self-deceit or from the arrogance of an over-theoretical mind, or from both combined. It is because the reader is forced into active moral judgements through being drawn into an elaborate fiction that the method is unlike formal philosophising; and it is because the reader is forced to judge in a self-conscious and contemplative way that the method may yield philosophical enlightenment. To put it more crudely, there are few abstract propositions in Fielding; he is a novelist and not a philosopher. But equally philosophy, and even profound philosophy, can perfectly well get along without abstract generalisation.

When Fielding theorises about Goodness and the 'Good Heart', he is, of course, philosophising in a much more formal and obvious way. But the significance of what he says on these occasions only becomes clear if one recognises that the whole novel is philosophy of a sort, and if one traces the implications of the theory of the Good Heart as they work themselves out through this mass of material. If the body of the novel and the theory of the Good Heart are allowed to fall apart each loses the significance which it bears in union with the other. The theory of the Good Heart can then look like no more than the claim that moral virtue is the mechanical outcome of psychological accident, and the painstaking construction of an anti-reductionist phenomenology of the moral life, which constitutes the substance of the book, can seem like puppetry in the service of moral preconception. In what follows I shall try to restore them to their proper unity.

II

Worry about the decay of language, and zeal for its restoration, were literary and philosophical commonplaces in Fielding's day. The 'purification' of language to fit it for scientific purposes was a prime concern of the Royal Society at its inception: metaphor and figure were to be eschewed, and all abstruse and complex terms clearly defined in terms of simpler notions.[36] This in a

[36] A statement of this programme, presented under the guise of a psychological description of the mechanisms of communication by means of language, can be found in Book III of Locke's *Essay*.

way is admirable, but it has its pitfalls. Hobbes' definition of pity which I quoted earlier, is in context part of a general project of redefinition of terms to fit them for use in the construction of a 'scientific', mechanistic theory of human nature. 'Pity' is here 'defined' in terms of simpler (or at least different) notions all right; the trouble is that the definition has simply abolished its ordinary meaning. If we live in a world where there *is* nothing but greed, fear and pain, this is all very well; but if there *is* such a thing as pity in the usual sense, then the net outcome of Hobbes' labours as purifier of language is merely that he has deprived us of any straightforward means of referring to it. Swift reacted with characteristic savagery against this sort of 'reform' of language: Sprat, Wilkins and Locke are guyed in the Laputan servants who, for the sake of scientific exactness in discourse carried around bags of miscellaneous objects which they could exhibit when they wished to mention such a thing in discourse, thus escaping that unscientific reliance upon the resources of a corrupt and enfeebled language which could not be avoided were they to avail themselves of the corresponding common noun.

Debates of this sort commonly proceeded upon the assumption that the way to purify, or to 'fix', meaning is to discover and state the correct definition of words. Among literary men the concern for the improvement of language expressed itself characteristically as an interest in dictionaries and dictionary construction. But the obsession with word-meanings and dictionary definition was not only a literary one. The theory of meaning characteristic of British Empiricism in the eighteenth century assumed that the word was the unit of meaning. To a word corresponds an *idea*, simple or complex as the case may be; and to define a word which stands for a complex idea is to break up the complex idea in question into simple ideas, proceeding by stages until we arrive at simple ideas like *red*, or *hot*, which admit of no further analysis and can be explained only by pointing to the equally simple and unanalysable experiences of redness and hotness for which they stand.

The philosophical and linguistic arguments against such a theory are formidable and nowadays generally admitted. A modern empiricist would take sentences, and not words, as the units of meaning. That is to say, he might wish to hold that sentences take their meaning directly from experience, in the sense that the meaning of a sentence can be regarded as that set of experiences which would prompt us to assent to the sentence as true;[37] but he would hold that individual words cannot be related directly to experience, and that the meaning of a word is determined by its use, or its possibilities of use, in sentences. And, of course, many philosophers would push this emphasis on use further; towards Wittgenstein's claim that to understand the meaning of a word is to have grasped 'a form of life', a whole social game or fabric of practices, and that because forms of social life ramify and interconnect, to understand the meaning of a word is to understand a whole language.

One of the things which I find interesting and impressive about Fielding's concern with the corruption and restoration of language is that his thought on these matters constantly tends to break out of the contemporary obsession with dictionary definition towards the conception of meaning as residing in use.[38] Reconstitutive irony in Fielding can sometimes be a very blunt instrument: merely a matter of juxtaposing a word with a parodic dictionary definition. Thus the entries in *A Modern Glossary*:[39]

HAPPINESS.	Grandeur.
HONOUR.	Duelling.
MODESTY.	Awkwardness, rusticity.
FOOL.	A complex idea, compounded of poverty, honesty, piety, and simplicity.

This technique is part of the stock-in-trade of any humorous columnist. But even here there are hints of something more. The learned terminology of 'complex ideas' in the definition of FOOL turns this particular definition into a point against Locke's theory of the nature of definition in general.

Locke's term *idea* is complicatedly ambiguous, as befits the key term in the system of a great philosopher who is at once

[37] An adequate formulation of this position would have in fact to be a little more complicated. See, for example, W. V. Quine, *Word and Object*, M.I.T. Press, *passim*.

[38] Glenn W. Hatfield's book, which I quoted a few pages ago, is excellent on most aspects of Fielding's concern with language, but underestimates Fielding's originality in this respect.

[39] *The Covent Garden Journal*, No. 4, Tuesday 14 January, 1752.

nobly muddle-headed in a very English way, and magnificently ingenious in inventing the endless turns and devices by which the numberless inconsistencies of his philosophy are made to fit together into a coherent, if ramshackle, whole. But, roughly speaking, an idea is the thought or concept which a word expresses. To define a word is, for Locke, to show what simple ideas enter into the composition of the complex idea associated with the word in the mind of the speaker. This, in effect, turns questions of meaning into questions of psychology. Fielding's point now, is that the composition of ideas in particular minds – minds which may very well be corrupt or ignorant – has nothing to do with the meanings of words. It may very well be the case that in many minds the complex idea corresponding to the word 'fool' is really compounded of the simple ideas *poor*, *honest*, *pious*, and *simple*. But are we to say, therefore, that that is the meaning of 'fool'? If so, we shall have no means of speaking of folly in the usual sense. In the minds we have been considering there is indeed no *idea* of folly in the usual sense. But that does not mean that folly in the usual sense does not exist but only those those minds are blind to its existence.

Fielding makes the same point in the disquisition on love in the preamble to Book VI of *Tom Jones*:

> . . . the truth finder (trying to discover whether there is such a passion as love), having raked out that jakes, his own mind, and being there capable of tracing no ray of divinity, nor anything virtuous or good, or lovely, or loving, very fairly, honestly, and logically concludes that no such things exist in the whole creation.

And later in the same passage:

> Examine your heart, my good reader, and resolve whether you do believe these matters with me. If you do, you may now proceed to their exemplification in the following pages: if you do not, you have, I assure you, already read more than you have understood; and it would be wiser to pursue your business or your pleasures (such as they are) than to throw away any more of your time in reading what you can neither taste nor comprehend. To treat of the effects of love to you, must be as absurd as to discourse on colours to a man born

blind; since possibly your idea of love may be as absurd as that which we are told such blind man once entertained of the colour scarlet; that colour seemed to him to be very much like the sound of a trumpet: and love probably may, in your opinion, very greatly resemble a dish of soup, or a sirloin of roast-beef.

If we read this passage in a Lockeian frame of mind, it may seem as if Fielding wished to claim that love is a Lockeian simple idea,[40] like those of yellowness or the taste of pineapple, which, because it is absolutely simple, homogeneous and without parts or elements, cannot be verbally defined in terms of other ideas, and which hence can only be understood at all by those who have had the experience of which it is the idea: who have for example actually seen something yellow or tasted a pineapple (this is why the blind man in Locke's celebrated example fails so miserably to define 'scarlet'). Locke's theory of definition, in short, leaves us only two options: either a word cannot be verbally defined at all, in which case it stands for a simple idea, or else it stands for a complex idea, in which case its meaning can be exhaustively defined simply by listing the simple ideas which enter into that complex idea.

The conclusion towards which Fielding's irony is leading him in the above passages and others like them is, however, that this Lockeian dichotomy is a false one. Love to Fielding is a complex notion: it is not simple in the way that a taste or a colour is simple, and indeed the whole of *Tom Jones* can be seen as an exploration of its complexity. But it does not follow that it is possible to exhaust the meaning of the word 'love' by means of a verbal definition in terms of simple ideas. Locke held that the

[40] This might go some way towards explaining why this passage has been read by adverse critics simply as an appeal by Fielding to the easy and irrational community of moral sentiments which his method allegedly required him to share with his readers. But most often, I think, such an interpretation has leaned on the first sentence ('Examine your heart . . .') and the Lockeian allusions later on have simply been missed. This is understandable: it is not entirely the fault of literary men that they nowadays regard philosophy not as a branch of literature but as a tangle of abstruse technical quibbles. But it does hinder the reading of Fielding, who in his day could assume a level of philosophical education extending at least to the main tenets of the *Essay* among all literate men and women.

function of language was to transfer ideas from one mind to another. Language cannot, in Locke's scheme of things, effect such a transfer in the case of simple ideas: I can only come to possess a simple idea through the experience of some corresponding set of sense-impressions. But any complex idea can be transferred from one mind to another by means of verbal explication alone. The difficulty Fielding saw with this is a quite general one, although Fielding articulates it only through ironic discussions of the meaning of particular notions such as love or honour or prudence. It is that in common life there are plenty of notions which, while they are certainly not simple in the sense (which for Locke is the philosophically fundamental one, and the one which defines his use of the term) in which the taste of a pineapple or the colour of a lemon are simple, are nevertheless not such that an adequate idea of them could be, as Locke would say, 'communicated into the mind' solely by verbal definition. Knowing the meaning of 'love', Fielding insists over and over again, entails being able to take delight in the good of others. This is not a 'simple' experience in Locke's sense, but it is necessary to have experienced such a thing before one can attach any meaning to the word 'love', since all the 'effects of love' flow from this experience as their primordial root. The man who knows only lust, calling lust 'love' when its object is what Fielding feelingly describes as 'a certain quantity of delicate white human flesh', is ignorant of the very nature of love, and cannot be helped to an understanding of it by verbal definition or explication, because any such explication, in order to get started, will have to mention the taking of pleasure in the good of others, and this is a phenomenon which those who have not experienced it will not only scarcely credit, but be apt to regard as a flat contradiction in terms.

So Locke's theory of definition emerges from Fielding's ironic tussles with it, as from recent philosophical criticism, defective on two counts. First, it teaches us to seek for the meanings of words in the accidental articulations of the contents of our own minds; and secondly, by offering us an oversimplified model of the relationship between simple and complex concepts, it encourages a heedless optimism about the degree to which understanding and enlightenment, at least in human affairs, can be derived from lexicography.[41] In crediting Fielding with this much philosophical perception I am not, it is perhaps worth emphasising again, crediting (or saddling) him with the role of philosopher, in the sense of one who employs philosophical modes of argument. His medium and his methods are literary. But the practice of literature need not exclude philosophical intelligence. Fielding is attacking Locke through irony and counter-example, not through formal philosophical discussion. But the attack is none the less effective for that, and that it is intentional is shown by the clues – the references to complex ideas and the man born blind – which Fielding left for contemporary readers to pick up. Unless we too pick them up we shall misread him.

At least what we have said so far enables us to recognise Fielding's dislike of dictionaries as something more than a quirk.

'If I was not as great a philosopher as Socrates himself,' returned Mrs Western, 'you would overcome my patience. What objection can you have to the young gentleman?'

'A very solid objection, in my opinion,' says Sophia, 'I hate him.'

'Will you never learn the proper use of words?' answered the aunt. 'Indeed, child, you should consult Bailey's Dictionary.[42] It is impossible you should hate a man from whom you have received no injury. By hatred, therefore, you mean no more than dislike, which is no sufficient objection against your marrying of him. I have known many couples, who have entirely disliked each other, lead very comfortable genteel lives.'

If we are not to learn the proper use of words from dictionaries, where are we to learn it? How are we to distinguish Sophia's plain and proper use of 'hatred' from the politic corruption of Mrs Western's use? Thus put, the question answers itself. We are to learn discrimination in the use of words in the only way in which it could be learned; by conscious and honest

[41] It may seem unfair to charge Locke with encouraging verbalism in view of his empiricism and his attacks on the verbal mystifications of mediaeval scholasticism. But I think the charge sticks anyway: Locke is, after all, one of the originators of the tradition of reductive analysis in English-speaking philosophy.

[42] Also lampooned in the *Champion*.

attention to the implications of using words in one way or another in actual, living contexts. What Fielding opposes to lexicography as a means of purifying and restoring language is his whole method as a novelist. The above quotation is itself an example of reconstitutive irony. We need not recur to another dictionary, a rival lexicographer, to discover that, and why, Bailey's definition of hatred is inadequate. Bailey's defects are sufficiently obvious from the nature of the sophism his authority supports in Mrs Western's argument.

To read through the bird episode is, in the same way, to become clearer about what it means to ascribe impulsive generosity to someone. From a negative point of view Blifil's parodic mimicry of generous impulse forces us, in the process of noticing the precise points of disparity between it and the real thing, to remember in some detail what sort of thing it is that enables us, in concrete situations, to distinguish between impulsive generosity and cold-blooded caprice. And by contrast there is Tom's ascent of the tree; thoughtless, and bound to come to no good, but free for that very reason of hypocrisy and calculation. Blifil's thoughtful observation that it was Tom's fall that startled Tommy into the claws of the hawk completes the contrast: impulsive generosity has received the only reward it is likely to get, unless tempered with prudence, in this world.

III

Irony cannot work in a vacuum to restore meaning and reveal character. The situations in which the implications of a diminished and parodic use of language unfold themselves, and in which we can perceive the slow opening of the revelatory gulf between the way a man talks and the pleasing picture of his motives which his talk is designed to foster, must be situations of sufficient complexity to allow ironies to multiply, and to unfold themselves simultaneously on several levels. For this to happen the characters must move in an imagined world which has sufficient depth and intricacy. The characters must constitute for each other a forest of constraints and hindrances, through and around which each character pursues his way and his interests as best he may, groping, stumbling, and in the process revealing his true nature.

This is the reason for the immense intricacy of Fielding's plot, a structure which has been admired for its mere technical ingenuity, as if it served no purposes in the novel at all. Consider, for example, the scene (Book I, Chapter 12) in which Mr Blifil breaks the news to Allworthy that his brother the Captain has succeeded in his addresses to Miss Bridget. The stage has already been set in Chapter 10 which introduces Blifil, the broken down, polymath failed doctor into Paradise Hall by way of an encomium on the magnanimity of Allworthy's treatment of such people.

> Neither Mr Allworthy's house, nor his heart, were shut against any part of mankind, but they were more particularly open to men of merit. To say the truth, this was the only house in the kingdom where you was sure to gain a dinner by deserving it . . .
>
> It is no wonder that in an age when this kind of merit is so little in fashion, and so slenderly provided for, persons possessed of it should very eagerly flock to a place where they were sure of being received with great complaisance; indeed, where they might enjoy almost the same advantages of a liberal fortune as if they were entitled to it in their own right; for Mr Allworthy was not one of those generous persons who are ready most bountifully to bestow meat, drink and lodging on men of wit and learning, for which they expect no other return but entertainment, instruction, flattery, and subserviency; in a word, that such persons should be enrolled in the number of domestics, without wearing their master's clothes, or receiving wages.

This passage is in itself 'mere' plot-building: it 'tells' the reader Allworthy's character, making him out a paragon of hospitality. Through several more seemingly meandering twists of the plot – Dr Blifil's theological debates with Bridget, the doctor's absent wife and Allworthy's knowledge of her existence, the Doctor's recollecting his brother the Captain and inviting him to Paradise Hall – the authorial voice rambles on, with measured patience laying out the ground. Captain Blifil's combination of Methodism and coarse affability conquer; the news must somehow be broken to Allworthy, and Dr Blifil, as pander and architect of his brother's success, is the obvious choice. Suddenly we emerge into dialogue, and the gallery of waxworks around which Fielding has been patiently conducting us springs into abrupt life.

One day, then, as Allworthy was walking in his garden, the doctor came to him, and, with great gravity of aspect, and all the concern which he could possibly affect in his countenance, said, 'I am come, sir, to impart an affair to you of the utmost consequence; but how shall I mention to what it almost distracts me to think of!' He then launched forth into the most bitter invectives both against men and women; accusing the former of having no attachment but to their interest, and the latter of being so addicted to vicious inclinations that they could never be safely trusted with one of the other sex. 'Could I', said he, 'sir, have suspected that a lady of such prudence, such judgement, such learning, should indulge so indiscreet a passion! or could I have imagined that my brother – why do I call him so? he is no longer a brother of mine –'

'Indeed but he is,' said Allworthy, 'and a brother of mine, too.'

'Bless me, sir!' said the doctor, 'do you know the shocking affair?'

Blifil's approach has been nicely calculated to secure his own credit with Allworthy – and his lines of possible retreat – by taking in advance the part of the latter's presumed fury, while at the same time placing him in a position to intercede for his brother from a position of general regret and commiseration when Allworthy's anger shall have died down a little. Allworthy's reaction takes the wind out of his sails. Allworthy then proceeds to preach an Allworthyesque sermon on the right of his sister to make up her own mind, and the folly of supposing that great wealth is necessary to a good match. The doctor, baffled, shifts his ground, but in his bewilderment shifts it in two different, though equally dishonest, directions at once.

The doctor accused Mr Allworthy of too great levity, repeated his accusations against his brother, and declared that he should never more be brought either to see, or to own him for his relation. He then launched forth into a panegyric on Allworthy's goodness; into the highest encomiums on his friendship; and concluded by saying, he should never forgive his brother for having put the place which he bore in that friendship to a hazard.

Allworthy's reply is lengthy. He begins by disclaiming any animus against the doctor, proclaims his certitude that the Captain is marrying for love and follows this with a general sermon on marriage which is worth quoting at length.

> Your brother appears to me to be a man of sense and honour. I do not disapprove the taste of my sister; nor will I doubt that she is equally the object of his inclinations. I have always thought love the only foundation in a married state, as it can only produce that high and tender friendship which should always be the cement of this union . . .
>
> To deny that beauty is an agreeable object to the eye, and even worthy some admiration, would be false and foolish. Beautiful is an epithet often used in Scripture, and always mentioned with honour. It was my own fortune to marry a woman whom the world thought handsome, and I can truly say I liked her better on that account. But to make this the sole consideration of marriage, to lust after it so violently as to overlook all imperfections for its sake, or to require it so absolutely as to reject and disdain religion, virtue, and sense, which are qualities in their nature of much higher perfection, only because an elegance of person is wanting: this is surely inconsistent, either with a wise man or a good Christian . . .

Almost incredibly, Allworthy has apologised for his sister's looks! The sermon ambles to its end, and Dr Blifil, fancying, to his relief, that he now sees with what sort of man he has to deal, has his face ready.

> Here Allworthy concluded his sermon, to which Blifil had listened with the profoundest attention, though it cost him some pains to prevent now and then a small discomposure of his muscles. He now praised every period of what he had heard with the warmth of a young divine, who hath the honour to dine with a bishop the same day in which his honour hath mounted the pulpit.

The most obvious feature of this dialogue is that Allworthy and Blifil are operating upon the basis of radically opposed social assumptions. Fielding has told us in Chapter 10 that Allworthy treated the learned indigent within his walls as friends rather than as upper servants, and, sure enough, he does. Blifil on the other hand obstinately persists in regarding himself as the fawning courtier of an oriental potentate. Each move he makes is based upon the assumption that Allworthy can be moved by flattery: his final assumption, natural enough, considering his own and the Captain's experience of Miss Bridget's susceptibilities, is that Allworthy, like his sister, loves theology and the sound of his own voice. But we know from other evidence that that parallel will not stand: when Allworthy in Book II, Chapter 5 is being roundly censured by Captain Blifil (who having won the sister is under no further obligation to respect the theological acumen of either her or her brother) for his alleged ignorance of the scriptural meaning of charity he bears the assault with his usual bland equability (which does not, however, prevent him ploughing on mildly but sonorously past the Captain's arguments to his own conclusion). Although Allworthy's goodness has something of the infuriating quality of Houyhnhnm goodness about it, it is still undoubtedly goodness.

That being so, everything that either Blifil or Allworthy says goes past the other. In a sense folly is speaking to folly, for Allworthy's generous assumptions about the motives of the Blifil brothers are as loonily inappropriate to the reality as Blifil's base assumptions about Allworthy's. Neither is speaking to the man in front of him, but rather to a straw man of his own construction. The disparity is comic; but it also serves to reveal something about the nature, or 'true meaning', of friendship: in Allworthy's purblind determination to find something to admire and to sympathise with in his guests' conduct we are given the moral converse of Blifil's determination to find some way of making Allworthy dance to his tune. Just because Allworthy wishes to like and admire, he is speaking from inside a conceptual universe in which the concept of friendship can be formulated in its full-blooded sense: Blifil, on the other hand, is speaking out of a world in which friends are people who have a use for each other. It is precisely because of the contrast with Allworthy's noble deludedness that each shift and backstep of Blifil's stinks of the drab 'realism' (I put the word in inverted commas because it leads him as much astray about Allworthy's motives as Allworthy is astray about his) which in his world passes for wisdom and prudence: it catches at the throat like sulphur fumes.

But, on the other hand, the contrast with Blifil reveals the ludicrous inappropriateness of Allworthy's patrician magnanimity. Like some amiably befuddled St Jerome in the desert, he wastes his sermons on an audience of wild beasts and demons. Allworthy introduces the problem of reconciling goodness with prudence which provides, from one point of view, the main theme of the book.[43]

Allworthy is the proprietor of Paradise Hall, which in a way lives up to its name and his, but which is also a place in which a child of good impulses is put out to school with dogmatic intemperance and barren theorising; in which innocence is regularly banished and plausible wickedness regularly passes for virtue; in which every cupboard has its skeleton and every conversation its rancorous undertones.

The contrast defines Fielding's problem. How can generous impulse be educated into virtue without becoming corrupted by the very prudence which it must learn? It is this problem which defines Tom's progress through the book as progress. And it is a problem which cannot even be stated from the point of view of the naïve intuitionism about morals which hostile critics have wished upon Fielding as his 'philosophy'. If goodness of heart is incorruptible and morally infallible, then all's well in the world and neither we nor Fielding need worry about moral philosophy. But as the passage we have been considering shows, Fielding knew very well that it is neither of these things, and knew therefore that he needed a philosophy going beyond a naïve appeal to the infallibility of generous impulse. What that philosophy was we shall now consider.

[43] The kind of prudence which Allworthy lacks is not that, for example which Captain Blifil chides him for not exercising in the dispute about charity in Book II, Chapter 5.

4

THE PHILOSOPHICAL CONTEXT[44]

I

We can best approach what Empson calls Fielding's 'central doctrine' by way of a consideration of his relationship to, on the one hand, the egoism of writers like Hobbes and Mandeville, and on the other to the conventional anti-egoism dominant in respectable English philosophical and literary circles in Fielding's day. The latter, which I find ultimately a rather depressing bundle of half insights and not quite avowed concessions, I shall call 'Standard Benevolism'.

Egoism is the doctrine that all men are wholly selfish all the time; or that no man ever acts save for the sake of some future state of his own (mental or physical) person. People, especially young people, often accept this thesis with cheerful alacrity, as though it were an obvious truism, or a piece of robust common sense. This ought to astonish us, if we consider the incredible generality of the egoist's claim. *Everyone, everywhere, all the time* acts selfishly? How could one possibly know? What conceivable mode of empirical inquiry could establish a conclusion of such summary and magisterial universality?

The explanation is, I think, that the egoist has up his sleeve one of those brilliantly general knock-down proofs which delight the heart of the philosopher and the sixth-form know-all, and that this proof is sufficiently obvious to occur to people at once, even when they hear the egoist position stated for the first time. The proof goes like this. To say that somebody, X, performed an action, a, of his own free will is to say that it pleased him to do it. But to say *that* is to say that X did a for the sake of the pleasure which it gave him to do a. But the pleasure X gets from doing a is, obviously, a state of X's mind. It follows, therefore, that X does nothing save for the sake of

[44] The reader may feel with irritation that this chapter has nothing to do with what has gone before. However I would ask him to be patient: he will find that it has everything to do with Chapters 5 and 6, and that through them it connects with Chapters 1–3, so that the book, if read straight through, forms in the end a single argument.

future mental states of his, or for the sake of future states of his body which happen to be necessary to the maintenance of the mental states in question. The argument is put succinctly by Mandeville thus :

> . . . in the choice of things men *must* be determined by the perception they have of happiness; and . . . no person can commit or set about an action which at the present time seems not best to him.[45] (My italics.)

It is, of course, open to the critic to object that even though this argument may seem to have no obvious flaw it cannot really prove what it appears to prove, since unselfish action is a matter of common daily observation. Against this the egoist has no option but to defend the force of his argument piecemeal. That is, he must take separately each example of putatively unselfish action which the anti-egoist produces, and try to suggest some plausible ulterior motive which robs the act of its appearance of unselfishness. Thus, to quote examples from Mandeville, selfless bravery in a soldier 'is really' vain glory and the lust for honour; modesty in a woman 'is really' fear lest the scabrous reality of her inner thoughts should be at any time visible in her face or her behaviour, and so on. Detailed debunkings of this kind, together with the coincident demonstration that 'vice' is necessary to the prosperity of a great nation, fill up the greater part of *The Fable of the Bees.*

> There is no merit in saving an innocent babe ready to drop into the fire: the action is neither good nor bad, and what benefit soever the infant received, we only obliged ourselves; for to have seen it fall, and not strove to hinder it, would have caused a pain which self-preservation compelled us to prevent.[46]

Discussion of particular cases along these lines is obviously going to be inconclusive: the anti-egoist can always think of another example, the egoist of another ulterior motive. To some extent Mandeville manages to rise above the welter of particular cases by postulating a general ulterior motive for all actions

[45] Bernard Mandeville, *Fourth Dialogue between Horatio and Cleomenes, The Fable of the Bees,* ed. Irwin Primer, Capricorn Books, N.Y., p. 192.

[46] Mandeville, *op. cit.,* p. 50.

apparently performed solely out of a sense of duty or moral obligation: pride. 'The moral virtues are the political offspring which flattery begot upon pride.'[47]

When the incomparable Sir Richard Steele, in the usual elegance of his easy style, dwells on the praises of his sublime species, and with all the embellishments of rhetoric sets forth the excellency of human nature, it is impossible not to be charmed with his happy turns of thought and the politeness of his expressions. But though I have been often moved by the force of his eloquence, and ready to swallow the ingenious sophistry with pleasure, yet I could never be so serious, but, reflecting on his artful encomiums, I thought on the tricks made use of by the women that would teach children to be mannerly. When an awkward girl before she can either speak or go begins after many entreaties to make the first rude essays of curtseying, the nurse falls in an ecstasy of praise: 'There is a delicate curtsey! O fine Miss! there is a pretty lady! Mama! Miss can make a better curtsey than her sister Molly!' The same is echoed over by the maids, whilst Mama almost hugs the child to pieces; only Miss Molly, who being four years older, knows how to make a very handsome curtsey, wonders at the perverseness of their judgement, and swelling with indignation, is ready to cry at the injustice that is done her, till, being whispered in the ear that it is only to please the baby and that she is a woman, she grows proud at being let into the secret, and rejoicing at the superiority of her understanding, repeats what has been said with large additions and insults over the weakness of her sister, *whom all this while she fancies to be the only bubble among them.*[48]

The vision of reprobate mankind, with one finger in its mouth, being flattered into witless virtue by the easy elegance of Sir Richard Steele's style is charming but not altogether convincing. What Mandeville is saying is that the *only* motive a virtuous man has for his virtue is a *foolish* desire for the good opinion of others. But if this is true it subverts Mandeville's intended point. Suppose that a saint, like Becket in T. S. Eliot's

[47] *Op. cit.*, p. 46.

[48] *Op. cit.*, p. 47–8 (my italics. To bubble is to deceive and defraud. 'A bubble' can mean either a fraud, or, as in this case, a sucker, gull or mark).

play, is tormented by the fear that his pretended love of God amounts in the end merely to spiritual pride. The fact that he can entertain such doubts looks like a point in Mandeville's favour. But if Mandeville is right why should his doubts torment him? Why should he not advance to the obvious Mandevillean thought that his religiosity stems merely from the flattery of parents, teachers and religious superiors, lose his faith and emerge into an amiable Augustan scepticism? An obvious answer is that he dreads the knowledge of himself as incapable of receiving the light of God. But the moment we give this answer we admit that a desire to receive the flattery of others is not the *only* reason for his pretensions to sainthood. If it were he might laugh ruefully at himself on making the discovery and proceed to organise his life in a way that would gratify more of his vices than this one. But, proud man though he is, he has also grasped the inwardness of sanctity and smelled briefly the air of heaven, and that is something else again, and not to be laughed off. In short Mandeville's appeal to pride and flattery, meant to explain why people should sometimes act virtuously without any hope of material gain whatsoever, makes it quite impossible to understand why they should ever do so, except on the assumption of an implausible degree of denseness and self-delusion on the part of otherwise intelligent and self-analytical men and women.

The egoist has the option of two replies to this. For a start he can deny that the hypothetical saint's anguish really arises from the feeling that his pride irremediably cuts him off from God, arguing instead that it amounts merely to pique at having to renounce the self-flattery which formerly accompanied the flatteries of religious superiors, nuns, clean young men, dissolute old ones, and old ladies in general. This has a pleasingly sceptical ring to it, but the edge of the scepticism is once again dulled by the extreme and entirely unempirical universality of the hypotheses advanced in its support. That what passes for spiritual anguish is sometimes, or is often, merely pique is plausible. That it is always and universally pique is hard to swallow. And besides the new explanation merely repeats the old, and leaves us wondering again why, if the saint's anguish is just pique, he cannot laugh ruefully at himself and continue to enjoy the besotted adulation of others. Because he cannot bear to become that kind of fraud? But why? – If Mandeville is correct and the love of flattery is the *only* motive to virtue or sanctity, he *is*, and is irremediably, that kind of fraud already. And to persons of that sort, as we see every day, the recognition of their condition does not in the end come all that hard.

At this point the egoist may as well fall back on his second line of defence. Granting that the saint desires something other than flattery, namely heaven, still his efforts to achieve sanctity, even such as they are, deserve no moral credit, since they are motivated purely by a desire for his own present future bliss. The desire to look upon the face of God is no less a desire, and as such destructive of all pretence to disinterested virtue, than the desire for flattery.

The argument, as arguments in philosophy not infrequently do, has come full circle. We are back to Mandeville's original knock-down argument, to the effect that no one can be held to act virtuously in doing what it pleases him to do. For the moment I shall not argue against this claim: I want first to examine it more closely.

It is clearly fundamental to Mandeville's position, which without it collapses into inconclusive bickering over particular examples of putative altruism. But it is not, as a philosophical doctrine, peculiar to Mandeville, or even to egoism. The doctrine that no man can be counted virtuous for doing what he enjoys or for acting to protect what he loves, *even though his act in itself might be considered morally right in the circumstances*, colours the thought of almost all writers on moral subjects in the eighteenth century. It forms the basis of a covert complicity between egoist and anti-egoist writers. I shall call it the *underlying thesis* of egoism.

I do not know precisely when such a doctrine entered European thought about morals, but its intrinsic character seems to connect it with the Protestant emphasis upon salvation by faith and inner grace rather than by the performance of empty, because external, works. Once we make the contrast between the external act and the inner consciousness of the actor the central distinction of morality, the attempt to define morality necessarily becomes the attempt to specify the conditions of a truly 'authentic' or uncorrupt moral consciousness. It seems obvious that such a consciousness cannot be selfish: therefore it looks as though we can define it by excluding from its description all motives to which any taint of selfishness adheres, and this seems to entail that a man who enjoys doing something, or who acts only to succour some object which he loves or delights in, cannot, or cannot only, be acting out of moral virtuousness.

I do not want to suggest that this is a silly or self-evidently preposterous train of ideas. On the contrary, I think it is one of those fundamental dispositions of thought which, because of their very seriousness and profundity, have a perennial attraction for us and, as it were, lie in wait ready to be stumbled upon by anyone who begins to think seriously.

But I think that it is in the end a false trail. It is not at all clear that, when we have finished excluding from the description of a truly moral consciousness all disposition to pursue or to defend objects of love or desire of whatever sort, we shall be left with anything capable of moving the will to action at all.

This is, of course, exactly Mandeville's point. If morality utterly excludes interest then it is (logically) impossible to see how anyone can ever be moral, since to act at all implies an interest of some sort, however feeble, in acting. Mandeville, in fact, far from being the genial sceptic he appears on the surface is at bottom a curious type of radical puritan; one who on logical rather than theological grounds holds with Whitefield that 'our righteousnesses in God's sight, are but as filthy rags'.[49]

Put in this radical way, Mandeville's and Whitefield's point may appear too bizarre and extreme to possess serious philosophical interest. We are tempted to dismiss it out of hand as a sectarian pose of merely historical interest; but we should be wrong to do so. Kant, after all, held not too dissimilar views. Kant held that nothing is intrinsically good save a Good Will, and that a will cannot be intrinsically good if it acts in pursuit or defence of what Kant called 'phenomenal ends'; that is, ends

[49] George Whitefield, Sermon XXIV, 'What Think Ye of Christ?', Works, V, 360-1: 'What think you then, if I tell you, that you are to be justified freely through faith in Jesus Christ, without regard to any work or fitness foreseen in us at all. For salvation is the free gift of God. I know no fitness in man, but a fitness to be cast into the lake of fire and brimstone for ever. Our righteousnesses in God's sight, are but as filthy rags, he cannot away with them.' (Quoted in Martin C. Battestin, *The Moral Basis of Fielding's Art*.)

like universal happiness, or the happiness of the actor, or national honour, or even the attainment of the Beatific Vision, which involve the bringing into being of some definite state of affairs in this world or the next. The Moral Law, in short, cannot specify any particular tasks or goals, the accomplishing or achieving of which constitutes the essence of morality.

What then, does the Moral Law command? Kant has left himself only one option. The Moral Law commands that we act solely out of reverence for the Moral Law. Since the Moral Law, if there is such a thing, must be equally valid for all rational agents, this command also gives us the general form of the moral law; the so-called Categorical Imperative, which in the simplest of the several formulae in which Kant expresses it runs: Act so that the maxim of your action could become a universal law valid for all rational beings. So expressed the Moral Law is purely formal, in the sense that it does not elevate any particular state of affairs which might come to pass in the world to the status of ultimate goal of all virtuous action (summum bonum). It is no more than an abstract principle of harmony, the harmony in question being that of the wills of all rational beings. It instructs the virtuous man merely to do nothing save what any other rational being could equally well do in the same circumstances. Even the reference to other human beings which it contains is contentless except in relation to the Categorical Imperative itself: a 'rational being', that is, is simply any being capable of exercising Practical Reason; of understanding and obeying the Categorical Imperative.

The notion of practical reason so defined serves Kant as a basis for distinguishing between moral action and action which is merely self-interested; between Moral Agency and the pursuit of phenomenal ends. Men are moral agents only when they act solely out of reverence for the dictates of the Moral Law: that is, when they obey the moral law solely because it *is* the Moral Law.

There is a famous passage at the end of the *Groundwork of the Metaphysic of Morals* at which Kant encounters a difficulty which he immediately confesses himself unable to solve, and which he identifies as the outermost bound of rational enquiry into the nature of moral judgement. The difficulty is that of explaining why, in the end, anyone should ever be

76

moved to action by such an extraordinarily abstract principle as the Categorical Imperative at all? Why should this curious, bloodless, near-tautology strike us as even interesting, let alone as morally compelling and the basis of the moral compulsion exercised over us by every other moral principle or consideration? It is a mark of Kant's philosophical stature that he sees that this question demands an answer; but he has none, except to say that it must be so, since the Categorical Imperative embodies the logical form of our ordinary moral intuition at its most profound and authentic. But the problem is not an isolated one. It is connected with the other problem, which Kant discusses at the start of the *Groundwork*, of how we can know whether someone has acted morally or not. For an action to constitute an exercise of moral agency rather than merely another move in the mundane and ceaseless pursuit of phenomenal ends which inevitably fills up most of our lives, it must have been performed solely out of reverence for the Moral Law. But how can we know that this is so of any act? Can I ever with confidence ascribe such purity of motive to myself, let alone to you? Kant to his credit makes no attempt to dodge the issue here either. If it is true that unspotted reverence for the Moral Law is what alone makes a man a moral agent, then it is true; and it makes no difference that we can never know for certain whether a single truly moral act has ever been performed, or ever will be performed, in the entire history of the world.

If one is interested, as Kant was, primarily in arriving at a criterion of virtuous action, and not, or only secondarily, in arriving at criteria for settling questions of psychological fact about whether in given cases virtuous actions have actually been performed, then this reply of Kant's is philosophically unexceptionable. In any case I am not interested in either of the two difficulties we have just canvassed either as offering, or as leading to, an objection to Kant's general philosophical position. My point is that these two difficulties reveal an underlying continuity of thought between Kant and the egoist tradition of Hobbes and Mandeville. For the discovery which for Kant constitutes a difficulty, or rather a pair of linked difficulties, is identical with the discovery which Mandeville brandishes triumphantly as a conclusion; namely, the discovery that a morality which is wholly freed from reference to concrete goals of action leaves us no way of explaining how morality can ever be taken by human beings as a ground of action, or how anyone can ever be recognised as having acted morally. Kant's moral theory is, indeed, the culminating articulation in the eighteenth century, of the liberal, protestant, individualist tradition of which Mandeville was also, in his way, a minor luminary.

If, hypnotised by the distinction between the empty pomp of outward works and a true inward virtue (which, if it could ever be attained, would involve the denial of all passions and desires whatsoever, in favour either of obedience to a wholly abstract principle of rectitude, or of a complete abjection of one's will and self before God conceived as absolute and arbitrary fount of Grace) we begin to conceive of virtue and interest as necessarily opposed and mutually exclusive principles, we shall find ourselves led in logical consistency towards a further curious consequence of these – only apparently abstruse and academic – reflections. We shall find ourselves beginning to feel that *relationships* between people must be discounted in any description of a truly moral consciousness. A truly moral man will do what is right whatever relationships he stands in to others: he will not unjustly favour a brother, or a wife, or a patron, and so on. I would be disinclined to denigrate an outlook which leads men to think in this way. It is because of this element of republican Roman Virtue in the liberal, protestant mind that it is half true that, as a Sikh once said to Dom Moraes, 'there is no nepotism in Manchester.'[50] I find fault with it only because, when generalised absolutely and erected into a theoretical principle it leads to the view that morality cannot, at the most fundamental level, have *anything at all* to do with relationships between men: that morality in effect springs from within the *individual* breast, so that the concept of morality would in principle be as accessible to a Robinson Crusoe marooned *per impossibile* on his island from birth as to an ordinary man in society. The oddity of such a view is evident if we reflect on the difficulty of giving an adequate definition of love or trust, surely fundamental moral notions if any are, mentioning only one man: but such things are generally forgotten when the mind sets out on its philosophical travels.

[50] In Moraes' book about India, *Gone Away*.

78

I can perhaps show what I have in mind by a further reference to Kant. The Categorical Imperative satisfies the demand that the fundamental principle of morality should be independent of human relationships. Armed with fidelity to it, a rational being can generate from it a knowledge of right and wrong in any circumstances without any consideration of his relationships to other people, except in their capacity as abstract, interchangeable Rational Beings, each of whom possesses the same total personal independence and moral autonomy, conferred upon them, as upon him, by Reason in the shape of the Categorical Imperative itself.

I have found this in the past, and to some extent still find it, a noble and even a majestic conception, only I do not any longer think it has much to do with the ultimate springs of morality. The point at which my doubts enter is to be found in Kant's defence of the doctrine that only acts done solely out of reverence for the Moral Law can be regarded as moral, or virtuous, acts. Kant defends this doctrine by referring particular examples of action to the moral intuition of his readers, and it seems to me that the sort of moral response which these examples must receive, if this mode of argument is to yield the result which Kant desires, is one which expresses the protestant distrust of moral feelings springing from human relationship to which I referred a moment ago. Thus Kant wishes us to grant, for example, that a butcher who gives fair weight deserves no credit for doing so if he has done so only to keep on good terms with his customers. At first sight this argument may strike one as profound and incisive; a moral scalpel slicing to the heart of things. But: I wonder. If we respond here as Kant wishes us to do, we shall not only be denying moral significance to the act of giving fair weight considered as a mere, 'external', performance; we shall be denying moral significance also to the fabric of human relationships in which the butcher stands to his customers.

For suppose that the butcher's reasons for giving fair weight are that he is fond of his customers, has trusted them for years, grew up with them, plays darts in the local with them, and so forth. And suppose, now, that this fabric of relationships deteriorates badly for some reason, say because of a poison pen campaign, and that as a result of this the butcher begins

79

cheating his customers now and again as a way of paying off grudges. If we follow Kant we shall have to say that since the butcher's moral impulses have not proved independent of changes in his personal relationships with the people around him, they were never *moral* impulses in the first place : that the butcher was never a moral agent (never possessed a Good or Rational Will, that is) but was just a sociable decent man.

But this too is false to moral intuition. Common sense makes us want to say at this point that the butcher *was* being moral when he formerly gave fair weight; that his being moral precisely consisted in his doing this out of fondness for and sympathy with his neighbours; that the fact that fondness and sympathy for others are intrinsically enjoyable states of mind in no way logically impedes us from saying that the butcher, being formerly in them and acting accordingly, was then a moral, or virtuous, man; and equally that the butcher's subsequent dishonesty in no way impugns the moral credentials of his former honesty : rather, it is just that love and trust have left the neighbourhood, taking, scarcely surprisingly, morality with them.

The moral intuition which expresses itself in this way is not the protestant moral intuition to which Kant's examples appeal, but an older one and, as I suspect, one which is closer to the central tradition of Christian orthodoxy. I think also that in entering the climate of moral thinking from which such judgements spring we have entered the moral climate of Fielding's novels: to this thought and to its implications I shall return in the next chapter.

Distrust of the moral credentials of the feelings which arise from personal relationship has another consequence. It leads us to forget an obvious distinction between two quite different sorts of desire, which for want of any readily available English terms I shall call *appetites* and *human needs*. An appetite, as I shall use the term, is a desire for some goal which can be fully specified without at all mentioning the conscious states of other people. Examples of appetites would be the desire for food, warmth, clothing, money. Sexual desire would be an appetite in this sense just in case it took the form of a desire to use somebody's body, without the slightest concern for any mental state of the person concerned, or even for whether or not they were conscious. Human needs on the other hand are desires for goals which cannot be specified without mentioning the conscious states of other people. Human needs include, for example, the need to be on a footing of trust and affection with at least some people, the need for someone to tell one's troubles to, the need to do work which is, even if only in principle, of some use to others, the love of company and conversation. These examples suggest that human needs are always amiable and perhaps that to be subject to them is to be in an intrinsically virtuous state of mind in which the natural flow of one's feelings will inevitably lead one to act rightly (this is, in fact, the gutter version of Fielding's philosophy, which hostile critics insist on attributing to him). This is quite obviously not so, as a moment's thought will reveal. The desire to have someone around upon whom one can inflict regular mental torment in small ways is a human need according to my terminology, as also are, for example, the desire to be envied, the desire to be desired and the desire to strike terror into the breasts of one's enemies. But none the less, morally ambiguous as human needs are, they seem to me to be essentially connected with morality, at least in a negative way: they save us from egoism. They lead us, that is, into connexion with each other, and out of that solitary egoistic self-absorption which would be a perfectly psychologically possible moral stance for a human being if all of his desires were, in the above sense, appetites. It is because we are subject to human needs as well as to appetites that we enter into a world in which moral distinctions can be drawn, moral problems arise and moral anguish be felt. If we wanted to solve the problems which Kant's moral theory leaves unsolved, of why morality should weigh with us at all, and of how anyone can be known to have acted morally. I think we should have to examine the genesis of morality in the situation of beings subject to human needs.

One of Fielding's great virtues as a moralist is that he is constantly aware of the distinction between appetites and human needs, and of the attendant distinction between someone who feels the force of moral distinctions, even though he may not act upon them, because he inhabits a world in which, for example, the claims of friendship can weigh with him as moral considerations because he has acquired the human need for friendship; and someone who, because he has no needs which go beyond appetites, has no grasp of the real force and weight of the concept of friendship, or of any other moral notion.

In Mandeville's mind, by contrast, all sense of the distinction has vanished. Human beings are bundles of voracious appetites and nothing more. It is easy to slip from thinking that a truly moral consciousness would be above being moved by its desires to the idea that all desires are equally temptations to self-indulgence and finally to the idea that all desires are appetites. The belief that enjoyment and virtue are polar opposites helps the transition but is not essential to it.

I have been trying so far to show that Mandevillean egoism is not an isolated curiosity of thought; that it results from pushing to their extreme logical limits certain tendencies in a generally liberal, protestant, individualist moral outlook which can express themselves in milder and far more conventionally acceptable forms, and which, for example, underlie certain moves in the moral thought of even as unimpeachable a moral eminence as Kant. We might expect, then, to find some equivocation in the rejection of Mandeville by the philosophical writers – with the exception of Butler relatively minor – who made up the British intellectual establishment in Fielding's day; and we should be right. Leslie Stephen, discussing Deism,[51] remarks that as the century progressed the orthodox divines who attacked the Deist pamphleteers became more and more imbued with their spirit, until Natural Religion came to seem a wholly proper and respectable theological pursuit. Something of the kind is true of the campaign conducted by respectable divines and moralists against egoism: the anti-egoist Bishop Butler ends by finding it hard to distinguish the behaviour of the intelligently selfish man from that of the man guided by conscience. I want now to examine this equivocation, mainly by reference to Butler's attack on egoism, and then to try to show how much more radical and intelligent was Fielding's rejection of egoism than that of the philosophical writers of his day.

II

Butler's attack on egoism goes initially to the heart of the matter. Butler does not waste time concocting awkward cases

[51] Leslie Stephen, *History of English Thought in the Eighteenth Century*. Chapter II.

and counter-examples to the egoist thesis: he goes straight for the *a priori* argument upon which egoism ultimately rests: the argument that no man can be moral because any man, no matter what he does, necessarily (unless he be under constraint) does what it pleases him to do. If this argument is sound the apparent diversity of human goals is an illusion, and all men have in reality a single goal: the generation and maintenance by each of a state of his own mind: pleasure.

Butler's counter-argument is that pleasure in itself cannot be a goal of action. To be pleased is always to be pleased *at* or *with* something: with the taste of the steak I am eating; with the success of my attempts to get the Parish Council to do something about the dangerous crossing outside the school; at the improvement in my friend X's circumstances; at the enormous size of the marrows I am growing on my dunghill. *What gives me* pleasure (the size of the marrows, my friend's success) is always something which can be distinguished from the pleasure I get from it.

Mandeville's claim, indeed, is that this is so, but that in every case it is the pleasure which is my ultimate goal: the thing, whatever it may be, which affords me the pleasure, is desired merely as a means to the acquisition of the pleasure it affords me.

Butler's point is that this claim of Mandeville's is self-defeating. If the gardener desires that his marrows may burgeon gigantically *only* as an instrumental good (only as a means to something else; that is, in this case to the acquisition of pleasure) it follows that he does not ultimately care whether the wretched marrows grow or not; and thus we are left with no explanation of why their burgeoning should afford him pleasure in the first place. Like the proverbial man who is only here for the beer, the gardener is in the garden only for the pleasure; but that in itself entails that he will not get very much.

Mandeville's argument, indeed, rests upon little more than a play on words. When I say of some activity that I engage in it because I find it pleasant I do sometimes mean that the activity would be of no intrinsic value to me if it did not produce a consequent pleasure. Rubbing sore muscles with embrocation after a route-march would be a case in point: I do it not for the love of it but for the sake of the pleasant glow and the easing of the ache which results from it. But more often I mean that the activity in itself is pleasant, and that I value it for its own sake, as an ultimate goal, and not for the sake of anything further which I expect to gain from it: conversation, listening to music or making love would be cases in point. Mandeville's argument comes in the end to no more than a wholesale, and illegitimate, assimilation of the second set of cases to the first.

By this simple, but shrewd and absolutely sound move, Butler shows that it is not logically inconceivable that a man should have as ends of action things other than states of his own body or mind. One result of Butler's argument is that it dissolves the apparent identification, which permeates the thought of egoist writers, and is the essence of the disguised puritanism which I remarked upon earlier, between virtuous action and altruistic action. It is clear that if Butler is right, one and the same action can be both altruistic and very wicked. A man who plots the destruction of another, not because he hopes to gain in any way from it, but out of pure disinterested malice, is certainly acting altruistically in the minimal sense that his ultimate goal (viz. the destruction of the man in question) is not a future state of his own body or mind. Of course it *pleases* him that the man will be destroyed, but that is only to say that the man's destruction is his ultimate goal, as growing marrows is the marrow-loving gardener's ultimate goal.

Having thus destroyed the central claim of egoism Butler goes on to attack the detail of the egoist case, and in particular egoist definitions of the passions which seem to offer us a method of debunking *en masse* whole categories of action. A celebrated example of Hobbes' definition of pity as fear for oneself occasioned by the misfortune of others. Butler argues that on this view fearful men would be the most compassionate, which flatly contradicts daily observation; and that hence, while such fear is often an *element in* feelings of compassion it cannot simply be identified with compassion.

When Butler comes to make positive use of these extremely powerful arguments against egoism, however, the results are curiously weak and unsatisfying. He distinguishes between, on the one hand, 'particular passions', and on the other two ordering principles, conscience and self-interest, whose function is to direct our choice between particular passions: to tell us which particular passions to indulge out of the motley collection which clamour for satisfaction at any given time. The particular passions include both those which refer essentially to states of myself, such as hunger, thirst, etc.; and those which refer essentially to others, such as the need for affection, trust, commendation and so on.

Butler has very little to say, oddly enough, about conscience. The main effort of his philosophy from this point on is to show that self-interest is consistent with virtue, and not, as Mandeville would have us believe, essentially opposed to it. His arguments take the form of showing that self-interest, which he conceives as the desire to satisfy as many of my particular passions as possible, will lead me to choose those particular passions whose satisfaction is consistent with the satisfaction of others, rather than those whose satisfaction excludes the satisfaction of others. He then argues that the other-regarding passions – love, friendship, benevolence, the liking for responsible social tasks, domestic affection, and so on – offer the materials for a more complex and harmonious ensemble of satisfactions than can be achieved through the pursuit of such self-regarding passions as lust, revenge or cruelty; passions whose satisfaction is likely to unfit their devotee for the satisfaction of any others, and whose enjoyment is, at least in a civilised community, attended with much danger and uncertainty. His conclusion is that the actions of the wisely self-interested man will be in most, and perhaps all cases, indistinguishable from that of the truly virtuous man whose actions are guided by conscience.

III

This is familiar ground, to the literary man as well as the philosopher. We have entered, in fact, the drab landscape of conventional Augustan moral piety. Like Shaftesbury or Pope, Butler appeals to the notion of a natural order which links self-interest and virtue indissolubly together. For Shaftesbury, the presiding genius of British moral philosophy in the first half of the century, the very notion of goodness is equated with the notion of homoeostasis: of what conduces to the stability of some natural system. 'We cannot say of any thing that it is wholly and absolutely ill, unless we can positively show and ascertain that what we call ill is nowhere good besides, in any other system, or with respect to any other order or economy whatsoever.'[52] Goodness in general, and moral rectitude in particular, is for Shaftesbury that which is necessary to preserve on one level the social order and on a higher level the entire order and constitution of the universe. Moral reason, on this view, is the intellectual perception of fitness or harmony in the social sphere, as the sense of beauty is the perception of fitness and harmony in the natural universe. In either case the perception of harmony produces in us strong feelings of pleasure and approval.

This strain in Shaftesbury's theorising makes him sound at times as if he thinks that conscience is much the same sort of thing as aesthetic sensibility, and in the same way an amiable natural gift[53] with which a man may or may not be blessed. It was no doubt this which led Hawkins to his contemptuous dismissal of Fielding as Shaftesbury vulgarised, although as we shall see, by the time Fielding wrote *Tom Jones* there was very little agreement between his morality and Shaftesbury's.

As the century progressed, this conviction of the relativity of goodness to the stability of the universal order becomes, as a theodicy, the idea that God's goodness is saved in the face of the existence of moral and natural evil by the necessity of these things to the universal order. As a theory of morals it becomes the idea that to be moral is, as it were, to go with the grain of the universe, the human nature of the actor himself being conceived as itself an element of the great system, in intimate interconnection with other elements. But if my nature as a human being is indissolubly bound up with the whole system of the universe, it follows that in general, at least, it must be in my interest to live according to nature: to cooperate with the working out of the universal order. Thus in Butler as in the *Essay on Man* the conception of morality as harmony and homoeostasis leads naturally to the idea that self-interest and morality are linked, or even the same thing as one another. As Pope says, speaking of Nature:

[52] *An Inquiry concerning Virtue or Merit*, Part II, Chapter 1.

[53] 'A good creature is such a one as by natural temper or bent of his affections is carried towards good.' Shaftesbury, *Characteristics*, ed. John Robertson, Grant Richards, London, 1900, p. 250.

Wise is her present, she connects in this
His greatest virtue with his greatest bliss
At once his own bright prospect to be blest
And greatest motive to assist the rest
   Self love thus pushed to social, to divine
Gives thee to make thy neighbour's blessing thine.

It is this outlook which I want to call Standard Benevolism. Standard Benevolists speak of the philosophical enterprise upon which they are engaged as that of 'showing that morality is consistent with self-interest', but the consistency in question is not theoretical but merely practical consistency. What happens in Butler's theorising is, in effect, that egoism, ejected through the front door by a series of quite serious and impressive arguments, creeps in again by the back in the respectable guise of a 'rational principle of ordering' and is in this guise comfortably recommended as a principle scarcely different in its effect from virtue; while virtue, by the same token, is made to appear as the prudent man's surest road to the maximal satisfaction of his desires. And while this is going on the questions of how we recognise the moral rightness or wrongness of acts and of whether a self-interested act can be *moral*, as distinct from in *accordance with the dictates of morality*, are shuffled away into the decent obscurity of an unopened file labelled 'conscience'.

The crucial move of Butler's which leads to this Pyrrhic victory of egoism in his thought is, I think, his decision to treat other-regarding passions – which I have called 'human needs' – as merely one more category of particular passions. The result of this is that in Butler's theory no one category of passions has any more intimate relation to morality than any other. The passions – all the passions – are related to morality merely as a range of options confronting Reason, in the shape of the two ordering principles Conscience and Self-Interest. Morality is Reason, and as such is opposed to the particular passions *en masse*, the latter being conceived merely as a sort of raw material which moral reason must discriminate and reduce to order. It is no accident, in short, that Butler has been seen as an English precursor of Kant.

In thus opposing morality, conceived as reason, to the

passions, Butler like Kant covertly acknowledges the underlying thesis of egoism: that a man who is merely enjoying himself – satisfying a passion – forfeits *a fortiori* the right to regard himself as acting virtuously, and the corollary of that thesis to the effect that a man can be moral without at all experiencing the feelings which arise from determinate modes of human relationship. Whether he is directed by virtue or conscience, Butler's ideal man is as much a solitary calculator and weigher of relative considerations as Kant's rational being; and the moment he departs from solitary calculation to follow, disregarding other considerations, the call of a particular passion he ceases to be rational and *a fortiori* moral irrespective of whether the passion in question is a self-regarding or an other-regarding one. Butler in short, like Kant, offers us a picture of moral thought as something whose purity is in direct proportion to the degree to which the person conducting it is able to rise above considerations of human relationship; and as something which involves the operation of some species of reason; although in Butler's case the space left for reason in the diagram is to all intents and purposes filled by prudence.

This covert complicity between Butler and Mandeville explains, incidentally, why Butler can make no sense of the notion of conscience: remorse is a feeling (in Butler's terms a passion) and not, except secondarily and indirectly, a principle of choice. But similar complicities between the conventional pieties of Standard Benevolism and the scandalous heresies of egoism are to be found everywhere in English moral thought in the eighteenth century, and permeated the intellectual climate in which Fielding was writing.

5

GOODNESS OF HEART

> This was the time when all things tending fast
> to depravation, the Philosophy
> That promised to abstract the hopes of man
> Out of his feelings, to be fix'd thenceforth
> For ever in a purer element
> Found ready welcome.
>
>   – WORDSWORTH, *The Prelude*, X, 805–10

I

Good-Nature is that benevolent and amiable Temper of Mind which disposes us to feel the Misfortunes and enjoy the Happiness of others; and consequently pushes us on to promote the latter, and prevent the former; and that without any abstract Contemplation on the Beauty of Virtue, and without the Allurement or Terrors of Religion[54]

Good-Nature for Fielding, means not merely geniality but true, or pure, love.

I desire of the philosophers to grant, that there is in some (I believe in many) human breasts, a kind and benevolent disposition, which is gratified by contributing to the happiness of others. That in this gratification alone, as in friendship, in parental and filial affection, and indeed in general philanthropy, there is a great and exquisite delight. That if we will not call such disposition love, we have no name for it.[55]

When one compares this with the elegant cosmic aestheticism of Shaftesbury's moralising, or with Butler's shrewd appeals to enlightened self-interest, it has a quaint and homespun ring to it. But the notion of pure love is not, after all, just something that Fielding made up out of his own amiable West Country

---

[54] Fielding, 'On the Knowledge of the Characters of Men.'
[55] *Tom Jones*, VI, 1.

head. It has a long and respectable philosophical history, going back ultimately, I suppose, to the *Symposium*, and it had been a commonplace of moral and theological debate in the preceding century. For example, it is the central pillar of Leibniz' moral philosophy, an edifice whose plan was never clearly grasped in England, despite the popularity of the vulgarised Leibnizianism propagated by Shaftesbury and the *Essay on Man*, and which is nowadays only infrequently visited, even by philosophers, although it remains an impressive structure. Thus:

> *genuine pure love* consists in that state in which we find pleasure in the perfections and felicity of the beloved . . .[56]

And here is the same notion in Thomas Traherne, whose view of the connections between love, goodness, felicity and salvation is virtually identical with Fielding's.

> . . . to be Pleased, and to love are the same thing. If there be any difference, the pleasure we take in any Object is the root of that Desire, which we call Love, and the affection, whereby we pursue the pleasure that is apprehended in it, is part of the Love that we bear unto it; the end of which is the Completion of that pleasure which it first perceives . . .
> . . . VERTUOUS Love is that which proceedeth from a well governed understanding, and is seated in a Will that is guided by Reason. It renders to all things their just Due, and is the Powerful Parent of all kind of Vertues.
> . . . GOODNESS is a vertue of the first Estate, a Divine Perfection in GOD by which he is, and enjoys his Blessedness. In Men it is an Habit or Act of the soul, by force of which they Love, and delight in all that is Blessed[57]

Such parallels, while they save Fielding the philosopher from the charge of what Berenson called 'the originality of incompetence', do not, of course, in themselves establish his philosophical acumen. For what exactly does the concept of pure love contribute to the understanding of the nature of moral virtue?

[56] G. W. Leibniz, 'Principles of Nature and Grace', in *The Manadology and other Philosophical Writings*, Tr. Latta, Oxford, 1898, p. 422.
[57] Thomas Traherne, *Christian Ethicks* (1675), Chapters VI, XI.

Butler would have granted the existence of pure love, but he would have assigned it to the category of particular passions. That is to say, he would have agreed that one human being can take pleasure in what Leibniz calls 'the perfections and felicity' of another. But he would have seen in this merely another mode of desire, having no particular moral value in itself, whose claims upon us on particular occasions must be weighed like those of any other desire upon the scales of conscience or of a prudent self-interest.

And at first sight Butler seems to have common sense on his side. We may reasonably doubt whether pure love always leads us towards virtue. If I become so besotted with one person that I neglect my duty to another, my love may be pure but it is not by reason of that virtuous. In the same way and for the same reasons one can find something lush, overblown and evasive in Traherne's celebration of love. There is something, it seems, too facile about Traherne's slide from saying that 'to be Pleased, and to love are the same thing' to saying that 'VERTUOUS love . . . renders to all things their just due.' The 'just due' of duty is obedience, but it is often unpleasant to have to do one's duty; and it is hard, therefore, to see either how love, in Traherne's sense, can function as an adequate motive to duty, or how a morality which turns entirely upon the concept of pure love can fail to sap our moral energies at times when duty, in its least attractive forms, must be faced. These objections are, of course, versions of those which Hawkins and Johnson have to the whole ethos of Fielding's work.

However, if we want to understand what Fielding has to say about the relationship between goodness of heart and morality, we must at least notice that he admits and does justice to both these objections. First, he makes it repeatedly clear that Goodness of Heart is not in itself and alone an adequate guide to right conduct. Tom's peculiar merit in Fielding's eyes, as he tells us expressly, is not that he always acted rightly, but that although he often acted wrongly he never did so without *feeling* the wrongness of what he had done and suffering for it. Moreover, Tom's wrongdoing springs directly from his high spirits and warmth of character: from characteristics, that is, essentially connected with his goodness of heart. Sometimes Fielding makes light of this:

> he had already been convicted of three robberies, viz of robbing an orchard, of stealing a duck out of a farmer's yard, and of picking Master Blifil's pocket of a ball[58]

But at other times he does not. Consider, for example, Tom's behaviour in breaking with Molly Seagrim, having fallen in love with Sophia.

> . . . the concern for what must become of poor Molly greatly disturbed and perplexed the mind of the worthy youth. The superior merit of Sophia totally eclipsed, or rather extinguished, all the beauties of the poor girl; but compassion instead of contempt succeeded to love. He was convinced the girl had placed all her affections, and all her prospects of future happiness, in him only . . .
>
> . . . At length it occurred to him that he might possibly be able to make Molly amends another way; namely, by giving her a sum of money.

Let us do the best we can for Tom. I am not much impressed with the critical or the moral case for dismissing Tom as a libertine. I agree with John Middleton Murry[59] that there is too much generosity, gratitude and general considerateness in Tom's relationships with women for him to be dismissed as a sexual imperialist. The fact that having enjoyed Molly's favours he does not follow the customary practice of despising her thereafter as a whore is a case in point. (How different from the chaste conviction of Pamela in Richardson's novel that fallen women deserve all the suffering that an outraged world cares to heap upon them.) Again, Tom is not only following his inclination in breaking with Molly; he is under Allworthy's express command not to visit her. And finally this present of money is not a contemptuous token of final dismissal : Tom promises permanent financial support, and, as we read later in the novel, the promise is kept.

But all the same: '. . . by giving her a sum of money'. I have heard it argued that Fielding has a bad conscience about his hero's behaviour to Molly, and that that is why he arranges the

---

[58] Book III, Chapter 2.

[59] John Middleton Murry, 'In Defense of Fielding' in *Unprofessional Essays*. Cape, 1956.

diversion of Square's discovery in the alcove behind the old bit of carpet. I think there would be more to this argument if Fielding had used a limper, blander and more evasive phrase: for example, 'by affording her that satisfaction of pecuniary interest which was, perhaps, all Molly had ever really apprehended from her connexion with him.' Fielding's actual phrase is too bald not to be intentional: the Good Heart is on the verge of turning sour.

It is turning sour because Tom, although he *feels* keenly the distress he has caused others, is beginning to get the idea that he can buy off his feelings with money. All Black George's sufferings, for example, not to mention those of his family, stemmed from the fact that Tom in the flush of the hunt would poach Western's land. The fact that it was an act of benevolence for him to sell his pony to relieve Black George's family should not blind us to the fact that it is only because he is Allworthy's protegé that he has the power to assuage his feelings of remorse with benevolence of this sort. And again, at the time of the pony episode he was a child: we now find him again trying to pay moral *weregeld* as a young man. A rather unpleasant species of eighteenth-century gentleman is prefigured in this tendency: an uneasy sentimentalist; a gutter-Shandean who catches each fleeting impulse of generosity or high spirits on the wing for the sake of the pleasant glow of human warmth which it affords him, and then tries to patch together the havoc which such behaviour causes by liberal applications of bank bills. Such a man would be rather worse than Western, since his impulsiveness would cohabit, however uneasily, with a conscience and some power of moral reflection, whereas Western is less a man than an example of Leibnizian *conatus* run mad, with neither foresight, memory nor self-knowledge; merely Impulse at full tilt.

Tom must be saved from this fate, and saved he is; admittedly by the Comic Spirit, but by the Comic Spirit functioning in this case as an agent of moral growth. Tom is thus turned out of Paradise Hall with no more than £500 to his name (which, thanks to the operations of the comic Providence and Black George, he immediately loses). And at this point Goodness of Heart suddenly and mysteriously changes its aspect. It becomes, not a source of warm feelings or of 'great and exquisite delight';

rather it becomes a scourge driving Tom on to do in the name of duty the very thing he least wishes to do, namely to leave Sophia for good. For once he has been cast off by Allworthy, then without money of his own he must either abandon Sophia or involve her in his own ruin. It is at the behest of his duty to save Sophia from this fate that he goes off initially to fight the Jacobites, an intention from which he is only turned by learning, through the discovery of the muff and the pocketbook, that Sophia has anticipated his efforts to save her from a breach with her father by herself running away from home.

The Johnsonian critic, if he notices these aspects of the book, must dismiss them as inconsistencies. That is, he must argue that Fielding has no right, intellectually speaking, to appeal either to the concept of duty or to the concept of virtue (conceived as something in potential, even if not fundamental, opposition to the dictates of the Good Heart) given the apparent dependence of his moral outlook upon a notion of love which has in the end more to do with pleasure than with duty.

The trouble with this argument is that Tom's sense of duty is intrinsically connected with his goodness of heart: it is not, as the above argument implicitly requires, something which Fielding arbitrarily attributes to Tom by an exercise of Narrator's License in order to give the book a conventionally acceptable moral surface.[60] It is Tom's love for Sophia which, appearing to him now under the guise of duty, commands him to abandon her.

The mechanics of this transformation of pure love into duty are worth examining in detail. Suppose Tom did not care that by running off with Sophia he would certainly condemn her to poverty and probably to starvation (a most likely outcome, given Western's frequently demonstrated intransigence and Tom's lack of any trade or profession other than the wastrel's and adventurer's standby of the Army). Or suppose that he managed to convince himself, in the best romantic tradition,

[60] Fielding, indeed, anticipates this objection in his disquisition on probability and consistency of character in Book VIII, Chapter 1:

'Our modern authors of comedy have fallen almost universally into the error here hinted at; their heroes generally are notorious rogues, and their heroines abandoned jades, during the first four acts; but in the fifth, the former become very worthy gentlemen, and the latter women of virtue and discretion . . .'

that they could live on love, or, more exaltedly, that their love consecrated them to a tragic destiny which it were better they should endure than drag out a life of mediocrity and thwarted desire. In either case Tom's love for Sophia would not be genuine love in Fielding's sense. For he would not be 'feeling the Misfortunes' of Sophia. He would be feeling the urgency of his own need for her and simply writing off her probable future sufferings as immaterial; or he would be feeling a certain modest pride in his own heroic determination to confront the destiny of star-crossed lovers in her company, and setting about winning her over to his schemes. And so, by virtue of the very fact that these considerations outweighed Sophia's probable future sufferings in his mind, Sophia would not be for him an object of pure love. She would be an object of desire for him in one sense of 'desire', true enough, but as Fielding incessantly emphasises in didactic asides, I do not *love* those whom I merely want to possess. Blifil, about whom there hangs a persistent odour of sexual oddity (sadism, together with a hint of a homosexual relationship with Thwackum[61]), also *desires* Sophia, in a sense:

... he had ... that distinguishing taste which serves to direct men in their choice of the object or food of their sexual appetites; and this taught him to consider Sophia as a most delicious morsel, indeed to regard her with the same desires which an ortolan inspires into the soul of an epicure. Now the agonies which affected the mind of Sophia, rather augmented than impaired her beauty; for her tears added brightness to her eyes, and her breasts rose higher with her sighs. Indeed, no one hath seen beauty at its highest lustre who hath never seen it in distress. Blifil therefore looked on this human ortolan with greater desire than when he viewed her last; nor was his desire at all lessened by the aversion which he discovered in her to himself. On the contrary, this served rather to heighten the pleasure he proposed in rifling her

[61] Book IX, Chapter 8: 'Mr Blifil took his leave and returned home, not highly pleased with his disappointment: which, however, the philosophy which he had acquired from Square, and the religion infused into him by Thwackum, together with somewhat else, taught him to bear rather better than more passionate lovers bear these kinds of evils.' I think the allusion is obvious, but it isn't important, and perhaps I am seeing more here than Fielding intended.

charms, as it added triumph to lust; nay, he had some further views, from obtaining the absolute possession of her person, which we detest too much even to mention; and revenge itself was not without its share in the gratifications which he promised himself.[62]

Blifil's desire for Sophia is a logical parody of love: something we can call love only by a corruption of language. But Tom's regard for Sophia would, if he were able to adopt any of the modes of feeling about Sophia which might enable him to pursue her even after he has been cast off by Allworthy, begin to decline into something softer and more sentimental but no less egoistic. As it happens, Tom's love for Sophia is a pure love. It follows from this that he finds pleasure, as Leibniz says, in her perfection and felicity, and so it is hard for him to leave her. But it also follows from the purity of his love that the prospect of bringing down poverty and perhaps even starvation upon her head, and of seeing her wither before his eyes, *really is felt by him* as unendurable. Fielding accurately, and I think movingly, describes the agony of spirit in which this leaves his hero, and I think there can be no doubt that what he is describing is the agony of a man confronting a strongly felt and very unpleasant duty. But clearly, as long as the purity of Tom's love – his goodness of heart – holds fast, there can be only one outcome to the agony: he will leave her. The purity of his love does hold fast and he does set off against the Jacobites. If he had not, he would *a fortiori* have ceased for the time being to love purely, by falling for one of the self-interested or romantic ways out which we canvassed a paragraph or two ago, as a way of easing his dilemma without facing it.

At this point I had better guard against a possible misunderstanding. What I am *not* saying is that Tom's sense of duty is merely a reluctance to connive at the destruction of an object that gives him a lot of pleasure; the same feeling, for example, that might deter a man who covets a priceless Sung bowl from stealing it on the grounds that in his haste he might accidentally break it. If this were the only sense in which feelings of 'duty' could arise from the Good Heart, Fielding would be open to the objection that the sense of the term 'duty' in question is itself a

[62] Book VII, Chapter 6.

debased and parodic one; and that since such 'duties' could only arise with respect to beloved individuals, such an account of duty gives us no way of accounting for public or civic duties; or indeed for the most commonplace feelings of duty towards those whom we dislike or who happen to irritate us.

This interpretation of Fielding is, I think, a misunderstanding, because it distorts the relationship between pleasure and volition (or commitment to goals) in Fielding's account of the Good Heart. The Good Heart is not *primarily* an ability to extract pleasure from the contemplation of human beings (if it were, the pleasure I get from seeing an enemy make a comic spectacle of himself would be an exercise of goodness of heart). It is *primarily* a motion of will: a commitment of one person's will to taking another person's good as ultimate in his scheme of ends or goals; as an end coequal, that is, with his own private good. The primacy of volitional commitment in Goodness of Heart is not something which Fielding expressly insists upon, but it is an immediate and obvious logical consequence of his formulation of the concept. I must, after all, have made such a commitment, wittingly or unwittingly, if it is to be, from a logical, or conceptual, point of view, *possible* for me to be gratified by contributing to the happiness of others, for unless I had made such a commitment their happiness *in itself* (irrespective of any further consequence which their being happy might have for me, that is) would be at best indifferent to me and at worst a source of chagrin. The 'great and exquisite delight' which the Good Heart affords its devotees, according to Fielding, is thus (logically speaking) *only* accessible to those who have, with or without knowing it, made the prior commitment of will in which goodheartedness primarily and fundamentally consists. What makes the pleasures of virtue pleasures *of a special and peculiar kind* is precisely their logical dependence upon a prior act of will whereby I elevate the good of others to equality with my own private good in my scheme of ends.

All this will no doubt sound very abstract and rather olympian, until it is connected with our commonplace daily experience of the detail of moral life. Once you do this you can see, I think, that Fielding's position is not only psychologically and logically sound and plausible, but much simpler than it looks when abstractly stated. The relationship between friends, for example, presupposes just such a radical commitment by each to the other's good. As long as it subsists this commitment makes possible the pleasures of friendship. But trust, openness, delight in the virtues and peculiarities of the other, the joy of being wholly understood and accepted; all these reciprocal joys of friendship depend, it seems, upon the original motion of radical commitment. For if the commitment lapses; if once I discover that my friend's happiness or advantage is after all something to be bargained away in favour of some more private pleasure of my own, then the friendship, though it may revive, is no longer quite what it was or its pleasures quite as unclouded. And if such episodes of betrayal recur it decays and dissipates altogether.

This relationship has an important corollary; namely, that unless a man is capable of making a radical commitment of his will to another's good, 'friendship' in the ordinary sense will be a meaningless notion to him, and by the same token the pleasures of friendship will be inaccessible to him.[63] Until he takes this volitional step he is, in a sense, outside the conceptual universe in which terms like 'friendship', 'loyalty', 'trust', 'betrayal', and so on have a meaning. And the same is true of other modes of relationships similarly founded upon a radical commitment of one person's will to another's good. Imagine, for example, a miner or soldier who lives out Mandevillean principles in the pit or in the trenches. That is, he does at all times whatever is most to his own immediate advantage, and deserts or sacrifices his comrades without a moment's hesitation whenever it seems prudent. There is a sense in which 'comradeship' is a vacuous concept for such a man. He may know, intellectually, how 'comradely' men behave: he can watch them at it, and he knows various moral 'rules' or 'principles' of comradeship: you are supposed to watch for your mate's safety while he is cutting in a narrow seam even if this means being a bit too near the face for your own safety, and so on. But he has learned these rules by rote, and they appear to him merely as external constraints imposed upon him by the society he is working or fight-

---

[63] Cf. Book XII, Chapter 5, on Mrs Miller: 'Every reader, I believe, will be able to answer for the good woman, but they must have a great deal of good nature, *and be well acquainted with friendship*, who can feel what she felt on this occasion.' (My italics.)

ing amongst: he regards them as irksome nuisances and holds men fools who obey them when they could avoid doing so. He has no 'inward' grasp of comradeship just for this reason: he would not 'immediately know what to do' in a situation calling for comradely action. And by the same token the pleasures of comradeship are invisible to him: he has no access to the joy of a man who sees his comrade rescued from danger through his risk and quick-wittedness. And therefore, finally, the notion of 'my own advantage' has for him a restricted compass. The goods he can (logically) pursue do not include the pleasures of comradeship. The only way in which he could begin to pursue those pleasures would be by making a radical commitment of his will to the pursuit of his comrade's good. That would make 'comradeship' a living moral concept for him, instead of a collection of external rules of behaviour learned by rote and observation of others. That is, he would begin to perform comradely acts not because he was trying to present an appearance of comradeship, but because they flowed naturally from his concern for his comrades' safety. And by the same token, because he had begun really to value his comrades' safety he would feel joy when on occasion one of them was saved through his vigilance, and enjoy the trust and mutual support springing out of such episodes. The pleasures of comradeship; a new category of satisfactions belonging to the class we distinguished earlier as human needs, as distinct from appetites, would have been opened up to him. But in order to achieve this extension of the range of possible satisfactions open to him he would have had (by a principle which is at once paradoxical and perfectly familiar and commonplace) to give up pursuing his own satisfaction *tout court*.

The commitment of will to the good of others which is the primary ingredient of Goodness of Heart can thus be seen as a precondition for entering upon moral experience in the full-blooded sense of the term. That step into moral relationship with others once taken, the pleasures and constraints of morality flood in upon the developing mind,[64] and moral concepts come

[64] Of course, we are here representing a logical relationship of presupposition between the concept of goodness, or pure love, and subordinate moral concepts, as if it were a causal relationship holding between earlier and later stages of psychological development. I don't think Fielding clearly

to be understood, through the experience of these pleasures and constraints as they work themselves out in the detail of real life, with their full and undiminished force. But if that step is not taken, the mind remains fundamentally outside morality, which is to say that morality remains something known only through externally observing its effects upon other people's lives and actions.

The bones of this theoretical position can be recovered in scattered and fragmentary form from Fielding's occasional and didactic writing. In the *Knowledge of the Characters of Men* for instance Fielding represents some of the modes of human relationship to which goodness of heart admits its practitioners as forms of gratification to which the good man has access:

> ... in this gratification alone, as in friendship, *in parental and filial affection, and in general philanthropy.* (My italics.)

Again, the impossibility of explaining ordinary moral distinctions to a mind which has not taken the step from self-enclosed egoism to regarding others as ultimate sources of ends is I think, what Fielding is getting at in the following passage, which we have already quoted, and which is frequently brandished as an example of Fielding's alleged anti-intellectualism and faith in the moral infallibility of impulse.

> Examine your heart, my good reader, and resolve whether you do believe these matters [that there is such a thing as disinterested love] with me. If you do, you may now proceed to their exemplification in the following pages: if you do not, you have, I assure you, already read more than you have understood; and it would be wise to pursue your business or your pleasures (such as they are) than to throw away more of your time in reading what you can neither taste nor comprehend. To treat the effects of love to you, must be as absurd as to discourse on colours to a man born blind, since possibly your idea of love may be as absurd as that which we are told such blind man once entertained of the colour scarlet: that

distinguished the two; that is why he is apt to regard good-heartedness as a fortunate but inexplicable mental endowment with which some people but not others happen to be blessed. Some critics have interpreted this as Calvinist predestinarianism; but Fielding is very far from Calvinism.

colour seemed to him to be very much like the sound of a trumpet, and love probably may, in your opinion, very greatly resemble a dish of soup, or a surloin of roast beef.

But for the most part Fielding's theoretical position is not didactically expounded in *Tom Jones*: the reader is left to extract it from the dramatic structure which it dominates. Fielding was, I think, quite serious in the passage from the preamble to Book VI which I quoted a few lines ago: he was writing only for the reader who could read *Tom Jones* as a complex dramatic demonstration of a theoretical outlook in morals. Empson was right: it is true that the book 'builds up like Euclid'.

To see *what* is being built up we must first get the overriding moral polarities of the drama straight. The book is not, as hostile critics have supposed, founded upon a central contrast between Virtue, construed as the possession of a native warmheartedness which confers upon the possessor a faculty of moral intuition which leads his moral judgements infallibly into conformity with the common sense of plain Englishmen of latitudinarian persuasion, and Vice, construed as the absence of the right sort of heart, a defect leading to Calvinism, canting hypocrisy and a calculating temper of mind.

In fact, I think, the book rests upon two central polarities. They cut across each other to some extent, and neither is remotely akin to the above caricature.

The first concerns the contrast between the mind which, because it has taken the volitional step into morality (the step of treating others' good as an ultimate end), possesses a full and inward understanding of moral concepts and thus feels the full emotional power of moral claims; and the mind which, because it remains essentially outside moral relationship, grasps moral concepts only in logically thinned, debased or parodic versions, and feels moral claims only externally, as demands issuing from 'society' or 'convention', to which a prudent conformity is often desirable in the interests of self-advancement, but which possess no intrinsic emotional power to compel obedience.

Blifil and Tom stand most obviously at either pole of this dichotomy. Fielding makes it clear at a number of points that Tom's motives are entirely obscure to Blifil, who regards him with contempt as a fool who can always be relied upon to sacrifice his long term interests to some momentary impulse, and who has formed this opinion of Tom despite, or perhaps because of, the fact that the latter 'really loved him from his childhood, and had kept no secret from him'.[65] Blifil's policy, in fact, deceives him (as Mrs Western's deceives her in other circumstances: in Fielding virtually the one advantage which the virtuous enjoy is that the politic characters pursue their ends by the light of complicated reasonings of superb rigour and cogency, against which nothing could stand were it not for the equally magnificent falsity of the premisses. The arguments of the politic lead with brilliant *éclat* into the darkness because the politic reasoner, in order to arrive at true premisses, would have had to look at the matter in hand by the light of concepts and assumptions which his policy itself leads him to reject out of hand as baseless and absurd, and which he could only come to take seriously through the experience of abandoning policy and allowing goodness of heart – in Fielding's sense – some say).

> Of Jones he [Blifil] certainly had not the least jealousy; and I have often thought it wonderful that he had not. Perhaps he imagined the character which Jones bore all over the country (how justly let the reader determine), of being one of the wildest fellows in England, might render him odious to a lady of the most exemplary modesty. Perhaps his suspicions might be laid asleep by the behaviour of Sophia, and of Jones himself, when they were all in company together. Lastly, and indeed principally, he was well assured that there was not another self in the case. He fancied he knew Jones to the bottom, and had in reality a great contempt for his under-standing, for not being more attached to his own interest. He had no apprehension that Jones was in love with Sophia; and as for any lucrative motives, he imagined they would sway very little with such a silly fellow.[66]

Blifil partitions Tom's possible motives between 'love', con-strued as foolish and selfish infatuation, and sober self-interest. He thinks Tom all too likely to be besotted over a woman, but supposes him not to be over Sophia (since he imagines him to be

[65] Book VI, Chapter 7.
[66] *loc. cit.*

still involved with Molly); while he dismisses him as incapable of rational prudence concerning money. Tom's real motives and feelings simply cannot be fitted into this parsimonious geography of the passions, and in consequence Blifil simply cannot grasp the nature of the threat which Tom presents to him.

Here again, it is worth noticing, Fielding is making play, in a philosophically subtle way, with the dialectic of knowledge of self and knowledge of others. Blifil knows *the contents of Tom's mind*, because Tom has from childhood kept no secrets from him. But he does not know, in Coleridge's sense, what Tom *is*; and he could not come to know this without coming to know what he, Blifil, *is*. Blifil looking at Tom through the spectacles of Blifil's habitual outlook on the world, accepted naïvely as offering access to reality, to what is simply 'before him', can know neither Tom nor himself, and so cannot in that sense know what is before him at all.

Tom Jones offers us plenty of other examples of the contrast between minds which feel the full force of moral language and moral experience and minds which do not. There is the contrast between the unfortunate lieutenant, in Book VII, Chapter 12, and his fellow officers; there is the honest Quaker in the same book, whose love for his daughter does not extend to wishing her happy with any husband save one of his choice (a theme paralleled elsewhere in the book in Western and Old Nightingale); there is Lord Fellamar's curious sense of honour, which fills him with consternation at the discovery that the fellow he wished to have pressed to sea is a gentleman.

Recent critics have noticed, as we saw earlier, that all these cases are linked by Fielding's interest in the corruption and restoration of language. But to dismiss a use of words as corrupt is implicitly to take one's stand on the correctness of some other use: to propose a standard for our adherence. The satirist must in the end, implicitly at least, commit himself to some values which are beyond and above satire. There is indeed a kind of satire which manages to meet this requirement by constantly shifting its ground, satirising sex from the implicit point of view of puritanism one day, puritanism from the implicit point of view of an amiable Chestertonian Catholicism the next, Chesterton from the standpoint of an implicit Marxism the next, and so on. Fielding has been suspected of shiftiness of this sort, but I think the suspicion is unmerited and rests on careless reading. The constant position from which Fielding attacks the corruption of language is that afforded him by the concept of enjoyment of the good of others, conceived as the central, dominating, concept of morality; from which all serious moral concepts and distinctions ultimately spring. To exhibit moral language in the fullness of its uncorrupted potentialities of meaning is, for Fielding, to exhibit it in its proper relationship to the exercise of Goodness of Heart; that fundamental act which breathes life into the dry corpus of moral rules, and which can be regarded with equal justice as the commitment of the will to treating certain ends as ultimate, or as a simple motion of the heart. Fielding is thus enabled to speak of morality, virtue and duty with simple and unsatiric seriousness, and is no more to be suspected of having his tongue in his cheek when he does this than when, as often, he urges respect for the clergy, and expatiates on the virtues of a good clergyman. This is why his repeated attacks on the corruption of language are something more than good occasional journalism, or even than an Augustan respect for sound learning (which is also to be found in him). They all mount up to the central monumental eminence of his theory of the nature of morality: this, again, is part of what I am sure Empson had in mind when he urged, in effect, that more attention be paid to the intellectual unity of *Tom Jones* and less to its surface appearance of picaresque diversity.

II

Fielding knew perfectly well that the pursuit of the enjoyments arising from contributing to the good of others need not necessarily lead to virtue. What he did believe, I think, was that the capacity and desire for such pleasures were, if not sufficient conditions of goodness, at least necessary ones. He thought, in other words, that moral growth could only begin upon the basis of some initial capacity for distress at the suffering of others, and happiness at its relief, but that a man might have this fundamental capacity for goodness and still not achieve it. Western and Partridge are cases in point. Western is a man whose impulses are by and large sound, but so vehement, and so little restrained by thought or imagination, that it is largely a matter of chance and external circumstance whether they lead him to a commonsensical goodness or, for instance, to the witless tyranny with which he confronts all opposition from Sophia to the course he has chosen for her. Partridge, similarly, combines a real capacity for generosity and loyalty in difficult circumstances with a servile self-importance which compels him to make himself the centre of attention on every possible occasion by spreading his master's business around half the inn kitchens in England.

Two traits distinguish Tom from these characters; the fact that he thinks, and the fact that he sets no limits of convenience or personal relationship to the operation of his goodness of heart. As the narrative proceeds these tendencies grow in him, so that we pass from the thoughtless boy who persuades Black George to pursue Allworthy's partridges on to Western's land, and then learns at leisure and too late the moral consequences of the act, to the man whose behaviour to Blifil at the end of the book seems, as Empson says, to overtop even Allworthy's wisdom and justice. It is obvious, I think, that the two traits are connected. Thought about the consequences of our actions is clearly going to be necessary if we are to allow goodness of heart a wide field of action: hasty or unconsidered acts of goodness may not only involve the doer in inconvenience or danger; they may produce results which goodness of the heart itself would disapprove. But clearly also the more we think about the moral and practical consequences of allowing goodness of heart free rein the more we shall fall into the habit of giving goodness its head, and of solving *ambulando* the practical problems that arise on the way. Tom, by the time he leaves the inn at Upton is deep in painful thought about the consequences and implications of giving rein to his natural generosity towards women ('gallantry to the ladies', says Fielding at Book XIII, Chapter 10, 'was among his principles of honour'. We need not suppose that Fielding is here cocking a snook at corrupt ideas of honour: he does that plentifully elsewhere, but in a different tone of voice). In this frame of mind he meets, after the adventure with the gypsies, Mr Anderson the highwayman, and instead of shooting him, or running him through, or simply taking him before a magistrate, any of which he might with perfect propriety have done, he listens to his story and gives him a couple of guineas which he can ill spare. Is Jones satisfying his own penchant for lordly magnanimity at the expense of the highwayman's next victim? Partridge raises this very objection, in the tone of disgruntled self-righteousness which the plain man reserves for deep moral subjects.

> And to be sure it would be better that all rogues were hanged out of the way than that one honest man should suffer. For my own part, indeed, I should not care to have the blood of any one of them on my hands; but it is very proper for the law to hang them all. What right hath any man to take sixpence from me, unless I give it him? Is there any honesty in such a man?

Tom counters with a *tu quoque*:

> 'No, surely,' cries Jones, 'no more than there is in him who takes the horses out of another man's stable, or who applies to his own use the money which he finds, when he knows the right owner.'

Tom knows his own past dishonesties as well as Partridge's, and knows what they have led to. He is far from condoning theft, but he is farther from supposing that any man has the moral right *casually* to adopt Partridge's high tone of judgement on another; for has not he himself been arraigned before Allworthy, unjustly as he thinks, cast off and ruined? Fielding's point is that this has not made Tom rancorous, or less good-hearted, but it has bred in him a good heartedness chastened by sober reflection. And so he listens to the highwayman's story with some feeling for the complexity and treachery of the vicissitudes of life and decides on balance to believe him. Moreover his experiences have given him a ground of sympathy for the highwayman which helps to evoke in him a general compassion going beyond the private and personal loyalties and affections – to Allworthy, to Black George, to Sophia – of his boyhood. The Good Heart is spreading its net wider.

Fielding tells us that what Tom learned through his travels and sufferings is something called Prudence. At the start of the book Tom is constitutionally goodhearted, but constitutionally imprudent, and it is his acquisition of prudence in the course of the book which constitutes the chief argument of Fielding's narrative. Fielding constantly affirms this; critics hostile to Fielding and favourable to Johnson's and Hawkins' view of him as assiduously assure us that there is no moral development in *Tom Jones* at all, and that Tom remains the same engaging picaresque scoundrel at the end of the book as he was at the beginning. There is, to say the least, matter for puzzlement here, and the puzzle revolves around the meaning of the word 'prudence' in Fielding's mouth.

Matters are not improved by the fact that Fielding uses the term 'prudence' in two senses, one pejorative and the other not. This, of course, is no more than to say that Fielding admitted a 'true' and a 'corrupt' meaning of 'prudent' as of other moral terms. But unfortunately 'prudent', a word which seems to have been, like other adjectives of commendation, on the turn in the 1740s, has not recovered from the experience. Blake aimed a passing kick at it in *The Marriage of Heaven and Hell,* and any commendation which it might express has ever since been tempered with a sneer: 'Prudence is a rich old maid courted by incapacity.' It is thus especially difficult for us to recover the pure and untarnished sense of moral commendation which the word can on occasion bear for Fielding.

The episode of the highwayman gives us a clue. Prudence in Fielding's commendatory sense, is in one level simply knowledge of the world: knowledge of the chronic fallibility of human judgement – even the judgement of exceptionally good and just men like Allworthy – and of the ease with which lack of caution, ignorance, or even adverse circumstances alone, can betray a man into ruin. Fielding's implicit criticism of Allworthy throughout the book is that he lacks this knowledge. He is too isolated, by reason of his wealth and his virtue, to grasp the full extent either of men's depravity or their subjection to the force of circumstances. That is why, despite his transcendent generosity of mind, he fails dismally as a magistrate in the cases of Jenny Jones, Partridge and Tom himself (and of how many others? It is no accident that Allworthy's reputation among the country people fluctuates between saint and fool). He is simply too easily bamboozled.[67]

[67] The name 'Allworthy' should alert us to this, as should the splendidly comic purple passage in which Allworthy is introduced by being discovered

Prudence in this sense *by itself*, of course, will not make a man virtuous. But it is essential to virtue that a native goodheartedness should be chastened and guided by this sort of prudence. For only if he possesses this kind of prudence can the goodhearted man exercise his goodness of heart without either bringing disaster upon himself or producing, through acts of impulsive and ill-considered generosity, results which are bad from the point of goodness of heart itself: which produce rather than diminish misery.

Talk of 'diminishing rather than producing misery' suggests a rather cold-blooded utilitarianism, of the kind that produced the reform of the Poor Law. 'Prudence' of that sort is not what Fielding has in mind. Apart from mere knowledge of the world, what Fielding means by prudence is the art of *intelligently* satisfying one's desires for the happiness of others, so that such satisfactions multiply and harmonise with one another. Doing this requires hard thought and ingenuity of a rather concrete and detailed kind. Had Fielding, *per impossibile*, been able to acquaint himself with the more vulgar and technocratically confident versions of utilitarianism, with their penchant for solving human problems *en bloc*, by arguments arrived at by combining the principle of utility with very large scale economic and statistical considerations, I think he would have found them repellent precisely by reason of their assumption of a godlike superiority and generality of vision. In thinking morally, Fielding would have maintained, we are required to consider, in concrete detail, the actual men around us, and not 'man' as described by some theoretical model of great generality.

Of course you can argue that this merely locates Fielding in a familiar eighteenth-century tradition of domestic, sentimental moralising of which Sterne is another great exemplar, and which, incidentally, breeds its own special kind of inhumanity in the form of a cosy and automatic opposition to 'progress' (to be found well-developed, for example in that late bloom of the

---

enjoying the magnificent view from his mansion: the very type of Shaftesburian man in whom moral harmony mirrors the harmony of nature. The incautious reader will no doubt take this passage in dead seriousness as a proof of Fielding's supposed Shaftesburianism, forgetting that Fielding constantly warns his readers that in nature no perfectly good (or bad) character is found.

tradition, Thomas Love Peacock) and, in the end, a refusal to take seriously any moral question which cannot be dealt with on a personal and domestic plane.

I admit the importance of this *caveat*, but I think Fielding can be defended against it. Fielding was not in fact afraid of confronting social questions of some generality, as his proposals for dealing with street-robberies show. And when we find him praising his characters it is, while often for their conduct as friends, or wives, or fathers, as often for their discharge of the duties of some public role, as magistrate, or landlord, or clergyman, and for the moral intelligence shown in the way they conceive those duties. And however much we need general social theorising (and I think we do) it would be hard to defend the view that moral claims justified in terms of the theory alone should take ultimate precedence over moral claims justified in terms of the way in which the theory is found to operate at the level of such mundane and concrete modes of human relationship and interaction.

My main point, however, is that Fielding, far from supposing morality to consist in obedience to generous impulse conceived as morally self-guaranteeing, supposed it to consist in the refining and direction of an original goodness of heart by hard and detailed thought of the kind which a good magistrate or clergyman must practise every day if he is to do his work well. This is the final sense (and it strikes me as a rather exalted sense) that Fielding gives to 'prudence'. It is by the exercise of prudence in this sense that the goodhearted man ensures that his goodheartedness never misses its mark or breeds monsters: that the good of others which he so enjoys is made to increase and to harmonise in different forms upon all hands.

Thus it is no accident that in the course of the book Tom passes from being one who merely reacts to events, or in so far as he tries to direct them does so in a stumbling way which produces as much confusion as good, to being someone who can direct events about him to good ends. The episode of the highwayman marks the turning point at which Tom, having spent the first half of the book careering from disaster to disaster, begins to grow up. From that point we follow him to Mrs Miller's house, where he finds the strength and the common sense amongst his other troubles, to engineer the happiness both of Mr Anderson and his family and of Nightingale and Nancy. If he falls into an affair with Lady Bellaston (and it is hard to think of any other practicable way in which the penniless Jones could stay afloat in London) he extricates himself from it, at the earliest opportunity even though this means losing Lady Bellaston's patronage, and even manages to avoid the temptation of solving his financial difficulties by marrying Arabella Hunt, despite the spurious moral argument that by doing so he would put himself beyond the power to ruin Sophia. He is becoming, in short, the man who can behave at the end of the book with generosity even towards Blifil.

Puritan readers of the book fail to construe all this as moral progress and development of character, I think, because they take Tom's initial moral weakness to consist not, as Fielding thinks, in his lack of prudence, but in his propensity to sexual adventures. For them, therefore, the whole question of whether Tom has developed morally turns upon the question whether in the course of the book he has learned chastity and fidelity, and turns dramatically, therefore, upon the final interview with Sophia. But Fielding plays down this interview. In conversation with Allworthy beforehand, indeed, Jones expresses something which it would not be exaggerating to call desolation at the loss of Sophia's good opinion, and forswears further infidelity. But the episode is lightly handled, and Tom does not seem to feel any sense of sin. He does not feel himself wicked or abandoned by God, or reprobate; he regrets his past peccadilloes not because he regards them as more than peccadilloes but because he fears they have lost him the love of Sophia. And in the event Sophia herself seems scarcely more scrupulous: her token objections are brushed aside by her father in full cry and an immediate marriage ensues.

The puritan critic feels cheated. He may feel like Kermode that Tom should have been made to confront, in a real act of incest with Mrs Waters, 'the awful judgement of principle exalted into taboo'. He will certainly feel that the real moral issues have been begged, that Tom has not changed at all, and that Fielding has merely glossed over the moral evasions and crudities of his ending with the conventional comic dramatist's trick of wedding bells in the last scene.

I do not want to undervalue the case for puritanism, in

criticism as elsewhere. You *can* read the book like that, and get a reasonably coherent and systematic interpretation. You will not be reading the book Fielding wrote; you will miss the full force of most of the irony and all the didactic asides, you will fail to get any clear grasp of the workings of Fielding's mind; but you can do it and still find yourself reading a coherent novel, although a fearfully diminished and mutilated version of the novel Fielding actually wrote. And if the puritan moral outlook, with its all-or-nothing contrast between sin and redemption, its identification of morality with naked Principle, its refusal to allow any moral significance at all to feeling or human relation-ship in any form, were the only intellectually serious and de-fensible way of thinking about morality, then perhaps we *ought* to read Fielding's book like that; for then *ex hypothesi* any other reading of the book would be built, intellectually and morally speaking, on sand. But I do not think that this is so. Fielding disposes of a tradition of thought about morals which is at least of equal weight and seriousness with the puritan tradition. Hence it simply does not follow from the fact that Fielding does not represent the ultimate choice facing Tom as a choice between Appetite and Principle that his ending begs all the moral questions or that Tom exhibits no moral growth in the course of the book. What Tom has to learn is neither the suppression of his desires, nor the consciousness that he is a sinful and reprobate creature because and to the extent that he is a creature of desire. We cannot say, with Mrs Chapone,[68] that 'Good nature, when it is merely constitutional, and has no principle to support it, can hardly be reckoned a virtue.' On the contrary, if Fielding is right, good nature is the root of all virtue. We cannot extirpate the feelings and desires which it comprehends – and these include sexual desire and the love of men and women for one another – without extirpating virtue itself.[69] The task is thus not to conquer desire but to direct and

[68] Sarah Chapone, in a letter to Elizabeth Carter, *The Works of Mrs. Chapone*, i, 48–52, quoted in Paulson and Lackwood, *Henry Fielding the Critical Heritage*.

[69] This fundamental point of disagreement between Fielding and the Richardsonians lies behind the contemporary dispute about whether fiction should make heroes of morally imperfect characters. Johnson thundered against anything that might show 'Good and Evil as springing from the same Root' (*Rambler*, No. 6, 31 March 1750). 'There have been Men indeed

govern it by prudence. This Tom learns and this fits him to be Sophia's husband and Allworthy's heir. In one sense Tom's reward at the end of the book *is* a comic dramatist's device for shuffling all to a hasty close: Fielding on one level intends us to take it as just that. But it is more than that. Tom does not merely become a rich and happy man; he enters worthily into power and magistracy; and the augury of his exercise of that magistracy is his treatment of Blifil.

---

splendidly wicked, whose Endowments throw a Brightness on their Crimes, and whom scarce any villainy made perfectly detestable, because they never could be wholly divested of their Excellencies; but such have been in all Ages the great Corrupters of the World, and their Resemblance ought no more to be preserved, than the Art of murdering without Pain.' Tom, though Johnson does not mention him by name, is an obvious target of this criticism. Fielding's reply would have been that good and evil *do* spring from the same root: that in becoming better men we do not lose our natural passions but learn to allow some – the various human needs arising from goodness of heart: friendship, charity, trust, loyalty, public spirit, and so on – to guide and direct the rest. But the growth of prudence is gradual and never complete: hence good and evil are mixed in all real characters. 'In the next place we admonish thee, my worthy friend (for perhaps thy heart may be stronger than thy head) not to condemn a character because it is not perfectly a good one. If thou dost delight in these models of perfection, there are books enow to gratify thy taste, but, as we have not, in the course of our conversation, ever happened to meet with any such person, we have not chosen to introduce any such here . . .' (*Tom Jones*, Book X, Chapter 1). The bracketed 'for perhaps thy heart may be stronger than thy head' is a barbed shot at those who think like Johnson. What Fielding is saying is, in effect, that it is not he but the Richardsonians who stand for emotional response in morals. It is an unthinking moral response which sees no middle way between total vice and stainless virtue: a response which has no time for any detailed study either of men's real characters or the concrete situations in which virtue develops or decays. The puritan moral universe is, indeed, one in which Becoming has been displaced by Being, except, of course, for the extraordinary and inscrutable operation of Grace.

6

FIELDING AND THE PHILOSOPHERS

I

We are now in a position to examine Fielding's moral outlook from a philosophical point of view, and to place him with respect to the moral philosophy of his period.

What Fielding has done, in essence, is to reject what in Chapter 4 we called the underlying thesis of egoism: the thesis that no man can be counted virtuous for doing what he enjoys. To be goodhearted is to have made a commitment of will; a commitment to taking other people's good as an ultimate goal of action. But to be goodhearted is equally to feel certain desires and to enjoy certain pleasures: it is because friends desire each other's good, for example, that they enjoy the pleasures of friendship. On this view, desire and enjoyment of certain sorts, far from being inconsistent with virtue, are part of the essence of virtue.

By conceiving of morality in this way, Fielding has also freed himself of the idea that there is a radical opposition between Reason and Sentiment, and that the main problem for moral philosophy is the problem of whether we are to locate morality at one of these poles or at the other. Fielding is often supposed to have deserted the pole of Reason for the pole of Sentiment: I think it would be truer to say that he has deserted the whole dichotomy. Disinterested love is a desire, and its satisfaction is enjoyable – indeed, as Fielding insists, the greatest enjoyment we can know – but at the same time disinterested love possesses just those characteristics of reason which have led philosophers to work so hard at the attempt to effect an analogical extension of the term 'reason' to morals. Thus disinterested love functions, with respect to my other ends and desires as a regulating principle, exactly as do the Categorical Imperative in Kant's theory of morals or conscience and self-interest in Butler's, for if I subordinate the good of another person to a private end of my own then I am *a fortiori* no longer acting goodheartedly. Again, the theoretical scope of goodness of heart is universal, just like the theoretical scope of reason: any other person's good can be an object of enjoyment for me, provided I am goodhearted enough. And finally, if I wish to allow disinterested love its full scope I must direct my actions not by appeal to the chance gush of self-indulgent sentiment but by reference to something objective and external to me: the real needs and circumstances of other people. If I do not wish to impose arbitrary limits to the operations of goodness of heart, therefore (and someone who does that will not long remain goodhearted) I must 'reason' in the perfectly prosaic sense of 'think hard' about how I am to put my goodness into action: I must learn prudence, which is the act of being goodhearted in safety and with happy consequences.

Fielding has in a way anticipated Kant: one of Kant's secondary formulations of the Categorical Imperative is 'treat every rational being as an end in himself, and never as a means'. But Fielding avoids the moral rigorism which Schiller and Coleridge disliked in Kant. Fielding is not obliged to define a virtuous action as one done solely out of reverence for an abstract and content-free Moral Law, and so he can do justice, which Kant, at least in the theory of the *Groundwork of the Metaphysic of Morals* could not, to the elements of feeling and human relationship in morality. He need not say, with Kant, that the more purely virtuous a man becomes the more he rises above all feelings and relationships; the more he returns, as Iris Murdoch puts it, 'with a proud shudder of rational power',[70] into the citadel of a moral rationality for which other human beings exist only as notional loci of a similar rationality.

Moreover, Fielding can offer a solution to the problem which confronts Kant at the end of the *Groundwork*, of explaining why duty should have any power to move us to action. If Fielding is right, duty has power to move us to action because love has power to move us to action. For a sense of duty arises when the pursuit of disinterested love conflicts with my private inclinations and appetites. Then what drives me on, as Tom is driven on to abandon Sophia and march against the Jacobites, is the knowledge that to cleave to my own appetites is to abandon to its fate the object of disinterested love. Tom chooses

[70] Iris Murdoch, *The Sovereignty of Good*, Routledge, 1970, p. 82.

to abandon Sophia physically as the better alternative to abandoning his love for her, as he would do ineluctably, by transmuting it into appetite, if he tried to retain any connexion with her.

It is because of this that Fielding can say in the *Essay on the Knowledge of the Characters of Men* that Good Nature 'pushes us on' to promote the happiness and prevent the misfortune of others, 'without any abstract Contemplation of the Beauty of Virtue and without the Allurement or Terrors of Religion'. But Shaftesbury is the philosopher of 'abstract Contemplation of the Beauty of Virtue', and the passage must prompt us to ask how far Fielding's morality was, as Hawkins supposed 'that of Lord Shaftesbury vulgarised'.

Fielding's treatment of Square ought to make us suspect Hawkins' wholesale assimilation of Fielding's morality to Shaftesbury's. Square's moral rationalism is guyed as sharply as Thwackum's religiosity: indeed, the letter which Square writes to Allworthy and which clearly redeems him in Fielding's eyes, is the fruit of Square's conversion to Christianity.

> the pride of philosophy had intoxicated my reason, and the sublimest of all wisdom appeared to me, as it did to the Greeks of old, to be foolishness[71]

Elsewhere Shaftesbury is coolly praised: 'The elegant Lord Shaftesbury somewhere objects to telling too much truth.'[72] But Fielding's fundamental objection to Shaftesbury strikingly anticipates Hume's general objection to moral rationalism: the ultimate springs of morality cannot be found in knowledge of the order of the universe, or in the perception of a Shaftesburian 'harmony' or 'fitness' in right action, because knowledge and belief are not 'active principles'; they cannot move us to action.

> Mr. Jones had somewhat about him, which, though I think writers are not thoroughly agreed in its name, doth certainly inhabit some human breasts; *whose use is not properly to distinguish right from wrong,* as to prompt and incite them to the former and withhold them from the latter.

[71] Book XVIII, Chapter 4.
[72] Book XIII, Chapter 12.

. . . Our heroe, whether he derived it from Thwackum or Square I will not determine, was very strongly under the guidance of this principle; for though he did not always act rightly, yet he never did otherwise without feeling and suffering for it.

. . . This principle, therefore, prevented him from any thought of making his fortune by such means (*for this, as I have said, is an active principle, and doth not content itself with knowledge and belief only*). Had he been greatly enamoured of Sophia, he possibly might have thought otherwise; but give me leave to say, there is a great difference between running away with a man's daughter from the motive of love, and doing the same thing from the motive of theft.[73]

Shaftesbury held, in contrast to Fielding and Hume, that virtue is a species of knowledge. Rightness in itself can be defined, according to Shaftesbury, as what is necessary to preserve the harmonious order of the universe. The attribution of goodness or badness to anything is always relative to some system or order of which that thing forms a part.

So that we cannot say of any being that it is wholly and absolutely ill, unless we can positively show and ascertain that what we call ill is nowhere good besides, in any other system or with respect to any other order or economy besides.[74]

Goodness is any trait in a creature which tends to promote this universal order. Shaftesbury argues that a creature can only be said to *be* good if the good which it does springs from its natural temper. When he is saying this, Shaftesbury sounds like Fielding : it is no doubt this which make Hawkins, and has made many other critics, equate Fielding's morality with Shaftesbury's.

Nothing therefore being properly either goodness or illness in a creature except what is from natural temper, 'A good creature is such a one as by the natural temper or bent of his

[73] Book IV, Chapter 6 (my italics).

[74] Shaftesbury, *An Inquiry Concerning Virtue or Merit* (Treatise 4 of the *Characteristics*) Part II, Section I.

affections is carried primarily and immediately, and not secondarily and accidentally, to good and against ill'; and an ill creature is just the contrary, viz. 'One who is wanting in right affections of force enough to carry him directly towards good, and bear him out against ill; or who is carried by other affections directly to ill and against good.'[75]

But Shaftesbury finds difficulty in identifying the nature of a good 'natural temper'. The natural temper of a creature, he argues, is a compound of its affections. He distinguishes affections 'towards private good' from those 'towards public good'. He thinks that the latter are more generally good in their effects, but that some affections towards private good are necessary to the good of humanity when pursued in moderation, and that even affections towards public good can be bad when pursued immoderately. There is thus something accidental and haphazard about a good natural temper. Having a good natural temper is just being so constituted by nature that the affections I happen to have, in the degree to which I happen to have them, happen to produce good effects in the peculiar circumstances of my life. Such an accidental goodness, Shaftesbury concludes, is not worthy of the name of virtue. Virtue must operate consistently, and by its very nature, to promote good: it must essentially, therefore, involve discriminating between the demands of different affections, and it must therefore be itself not an affection but a species of thought or reason.

Virtue in this sense is in one sense an affection, but a second-order one: an affection 'towards those very affections themselves, which have been already felt, and are now become the subject of a new liking or dislike'.[76]

Thus the several motions, inclinations, passions, dispositions and consequent carriage and behaviour of creatures in the various parts of life, being in several views or perspectives represented to the mind, which readily discerns the good and ill towards the species or public, there arises a new trial or exercise of the heart, which must either rightly and soundly affect what is just and right, and disaffect what is contrary,

[75] *Op. cit.*, Part II, Section II.
[76] *Op. cit.*, Part II, Section III.

or corruptly affect what is ill and disaffect what is worthy and good.

And in this case alone it is we call any creature worthy or virtuous, when it can have the notion of a public interest, and can attain the speculation or science of what is morally good or ill, admirable or blameable, right or wrong. For though we may call an ill horse vicious, yet we never say of a good one, nor of any mere beast, idiot, or changeling, though ever so good-natured, that he is worthy or virtuous.[77]

This is very close to Hawkins, but very far from Fielding. Like Hawkins, Shaftesbury holds that 'the virtue of a horse' is not virtue because it springs from natural constitution and not from reflection. But unlike Hawkins, Shaftesbury makes virtue consist not in willed obedience to an externally imposed moral law but in the ability to experience not just primary affections, towards food, or women, or the good of others, but a curious category of second-order affections: affections towards affections. Shaftesbury is in fact assimilating moral judgement to the model of certain sorts of aesthetic judgement: just as we discriminate and prefer harmony to discord in music, so the moral man takes a large and considered view of his own and others' affections, and makes objects of admiration of those whose pursuit tends to produce consequences favourable to universal concord and harmony.

But what is it to 'affect' one of my affections on perceiving it to be in harmony with the order of the universe? Shaftesbury clearly means to define virtue in terms of the affecting of affections, and if the definition is really to clarify the nature of virtue it ought to be clear from the definition why virtue makes us do one thing rather than another. But it is not. 'Affecting' an affection, from the point of view of a clear knowledge of the consequences of pursuing it, may simply mean indulging a disinterested quasi-aesthetic admiration of the way in which those consequences fit harmoniously into the general order of the universe. And such admiration need not commit the person who feels it to favouring the affection in question if it happens to conflict with stronger affections, towards lust or revenge, for example. Of course a *virtuous* man will, no doubt, actually

[77] loc. cit.

118

perform the action which produces that sort of quasi-aesthetic admiration in him when viewed dispassionately and at large. But this is a *petitio principii*: Shaftesbury is supposed to be telling us not *how* virtuous men behave, for that we know, but what virtue is.

What is distinctive in his theory, and might be supposed to provide an answer to this question, is the idea that virtue is the perception of the fitness of right action with respect to the moral order of the universe. Hume's retort to this, which as we have seen was also Fielding's was short and conclusive: how can a mere *perception*, of harmony or of anything else, move me to action? That virtuous action promotes universal concord is, if it is true, a fact about the universe; but to know a fact, to know that something is the case, is not in itself to have a motive for action. I can always say 'so what', and do what I was going to do in any case. Admittedly a virtuous man will not say 'so what' – but this is merely to grant that virtue must be an 'active principle'.

In other words it must belong in the category of Shaftesbury's first-order affections; not in the further category of second-order quasi-aesthetic 'affections' which he erects upon the back of the first. Shaftesbury cannot place it there because, in brief, he assumes that all affections falling into that category are appetites, and thus that they have no essential connection with right action because they have built into them no element of reflection or principle of rational discrimination. He has accepted the underlying thesis of egoism: the doctrines, which haunted the age, of the radical incompatibility of virtue and natural affection, of reason and sentiment.

Fielding, as we have seen, being armed with an account of the genesis of virtue in a Goodness of Heart which is as intrinsically volitional and ratiocinative as it is natural, appetitive and impulsive, is able to pass between the horns of these dichotomies. This alone should prevent us identifying him as a Shaftesburian.

Fielding, in short, contrary so far as I can make out to most critical opinion, is neither philosophically naïve nor philosophically an uncritical child of his age. The deft and terse way in which he distances himself from alternative points of view in his brief polemical adumbrations of the nature of goodness shows perfectly well that he knew what the moral theorists of his age were saying and how his own position differed from theirs. And his mind in these matters is fundamentally alien to the Augustan concensus of opinion which reconciled morality and self-interest, human suffering and the will of God, in a vision of ultimate order and harmony visible only to the eye of faith or of rational speculation. His vision is less cerebral and more subtle. In its emphasis on virtue as an active principle and on the unity of natural feeling and morality it links him, via Hume, with the Romantics. In its conviction that virtue is not the rejection of created things but the right enjoyment of created things it links him with Traherne and English mysticism and with a tradition of Christian orthodoxy which, although certain aspects of it were maintained by latitudinarian divines like Barrow and Hoadley,[78] whom Fielding admired, did not find fertile soil in Fielding's century.

II

There are a set of religious, or rather moral writers, who teach that virtue is the certain road to happiness and vice to misery, in this world. A very wholesome and conformable doctrine, and to which we have but one objection, namely, that it is not true.[79]

So much for Butler's solution to the problem of 'reconciling' self-interest and morality. Butler's 'self-love' is concerned with the economy of gratifications: the self-interested man so acts as to secure for himself the largest number of gratifications over the longest possible run of time: hence, according to Butler, if he is rational he will choose gratifications which, like that of benevolence, harmonise with many other gratifications (such as enjoying the security and respect which a grateful community affords to public benefactors) and eschew gratifications, like that of giving way to murderous rage, for example, whose enjoyment must place many other gratifications beyond his reach. And hence,

Conscience and self-love, if we understand our true happiness, always lead us the same way. Duty and interest are perfectly

[78] For Fielding's connexion with the latitudinarians see Martin C. Battestin's excellent book, *The Moral Basis of Fielding's Art.*

[79] *Tom Jones*, Book XV, Chapter 1.

coincident: for the most part in this world, but entirely and in every instance if we take in the future, and the whole; this being implied in the notion of a good and perfect administration of things.[80]

It may be true that virtue is in some way or other in accord with self-interest in some sense or other of that term: I think myself that it probably is. But this is merely to say that the idea is a sort of philosophical blank cheque which, properly filled in, might pass muster at some as yet unidentified doctrinal bank. Butler's way of filling it in seems to me to involve, on the one hand, an uncharacteristically Panglossian complacency about the distribution of rewards in this world (had Butler never read Ecclesiastes?), and on the other a curious blindness to the radical disparity between the state of mind of a man acting out of virtue and a man acting out of Butlerian self-love. Even if it were true that a man might, by acting as a virtuous man might act, maximise the number of his gratifications, he would by the very fact of acting in that way *for that reason* be turning his back on the possibility of actually *being* virtuous. This throws doubt on the purpose and likely effects of Butler's arguments. They are supposed to draw men to virtue by showing that virtue is consistent with self-interest. But anyone who was actually moved *by Butler's arguments* to act virtuously would by that very fact, it seems, be choosing the outer shadow rather than the inner substance of virtue. And that in turn must make us wonder whether a man motivated solely by Butlerian self-love could really taste the pleasures of virtue. If my mind is filled with the whir of a felicific adding machine, endlessly totting up sums of anticipated gratification against debits of inconvenience in order to arrive at a credit balance, how can I take, for example, the alarming step of committing myself come what may to another person, let alone enjoy it?[81] But that seems to cast the whole Butlerian project of reconciling virtue and

[80] Joseph Butler, Bishop of Durham, *Fifteen Sermons preached at the Rolls Chapel* (1723), Sermon III.
[81] Cf. Eliot in *The Waste Land*, V:
> The awful daring of a moment's surrender
> Which an age of prudence can never retract
> By this, and this only, we have existed

self-interest into doubt: for a pleasure which is by its nature invisible to self-interest cannot be taken into account in its calculations.

Nevertheless Butler's arguments were very popular, and by the time Fielding came to write *Tom Jones* they were a part of received wisdom. They do not enjoy that status today, though views of the same general sort are common enough, and a modern reader can read *Tom Jones* without noticing Fielding's running engagement with them. But if one has had to think one's way through them the passage from Book XV quoted at the head of this section strikes with marvellous force and freshness upon the mind. In two sentences Fielding dissolves the whole shoddy fabric of complacency and bad reasoning.

Fielding holds consistently throughout his writings that to be virtuous is to live dangerously. The exercise of goodness of heart, though its pleasures are unmatched, is unsafe. The theatrical ending of *Tom Jones*, with deathbed revelations, sudden reversals and happy coincidences, is designed to make us acutely aware of this. Fielding wishes us, while rejoicing at Tom's success, to be uncomfortably conscious of the fact that he owes it to the Providence which reigns over comedy: that in real life Blifil would have ended as master of Paradise Hall and husband and gaoler of Sophia.

By the same token, the wisest course open to Butlerian prudence, which seeks merely to maximise the number of its gratifications, is not to practise virtue but to cloak malice and self-seeking in a hypocritical semblance of virtue. Blifil and Wild exemplify prudence of this sort, as do a host of minor characters. They are death's heads which stare blankly back, in the mirror of Fielding's creative imagination, at the plump and cheerful features of the Rationally Self-Interested Man celebrated by orthodox moralists.

What Fielding has seen, in short, is that there can be no question of reconciling morality and self-interest if self-interest is taken to mean, as Butler took it to mean, the rational calculation of maximal gratification. All such calculations involve sacrificing one interest to obtain the satisfaction of another: but to be moral, according to Fielding is to have committed oneself to objects of desire which can never (except at the cost of ceasing to be moral) be bartered off against other gains. I cannot *seriously* raise the question, for example, of whether I shall obtain more gratification from advancing my friend's interests, or from sacrificing them to secure my own promotion or emolument, without *de facto* ceasing to be his friend, and this remains true, *pace* Butler, even in the unlikely event of the world's being so constituted that the calculation always *in fact* comes out with a credit balance on the side of friendship and a debit balance on the side of betrayal. Friendship, and morality in general, is *intrinsically* alien to the calculation of self-interest. And that, of course, is why Fielding places the Good Heart at the core of morality. The goodhearted man, by taking pleasure in the happiness of others, commits himself to ends whose pursuit may conflict with his own happiness, and which he is not free to barter off against other satisfactions in the general post of self-interested calculation. He tears down the walls of caution which protect the freely calculating egoist, gives hostages to accident and fate and lays himself open to betrayal in his turn. He behaves, in fact, like a fool: small wonder, says Fielding, that he so often ends in poverty or on the gallows.

In short, the goodhearted man has cut himself off from prudence, if prudence means the rational calculation of self-interest. That is why he stands so much in need of prudence of another sort: but that we have already discussed.

III

We are led back naturally at this point to Fielding's relationship to Mandeville. It is worth remarking that Fielding very often writes about moral hypocrisy in a startlingly Mandevillean vein. For example his diatribes on the meaning which 'love' bears among town wits (love is that sentiment which a hungry man feels towards a plate of roast beef) have an authentic Mandevillean venom, and his treatment of the chastity of Laetitia Snap or Lady Bellaston might have been lifted wholesale from the passages on chastity in Mandeville's defensive notes on *The Grumbling Hive*. He is constantly aware – indeed it is a central theme of both *Tom Jones* and *Jonathan Wild* – that overt virtue is very often merely the mask of vice.[82] And yet at the same

[82] Thus see, for example, *An Essay on the Knowledge of the Characters of Men*, *Works* Henley edn., v. XIV, p. 283: 'Thus, while the crafty and designing

time Fielding presents us with cases of extraordinary altruism, such as Tom's handing over of Lady Bellaston's £50, practically all the money he has in the world, to Mrs Miller for the relief of her cousin the 'highwayman' and his destitute family. We do not need to have read Mandeville to be primed to shout 'escapist fantasy!' here: it will do very well to have read other passages of Fielding. And yet such protests die on our lips: the episode is, oddly enough, completely convincing. Now, why is this so?

Partly, I think, it is because when the egoist is confronted by particular cases of altruism he can advance his case only by suggesting possible discreditable ulterior motives; and this is a procedure which it is much easier to carry out in the rarefied air of a philosophy tutorial, where exemplary cases are barely sketched out with a minimum of contextual information, than in a novel, where contextual information can be deployed much more fully. Fielding is well aware of this, and it is part of the mechanism by which he establishes the concrete reality of Tom's altruism.

In the case of Tom's donating his £50 for the succour of the highwayman and his family, the most obvious ulterior motive for the egoist to postulate is the love of moral self-congratulation: pharisaical pride. But to love the satisfaction of pharisaical pride is *a fortiori* to love one's person and one's comfortable circumstances: such pride is a rather delicate luxury. Common sense would have given Mrs Miller £10. This would have purchased enough moral self-congratulation to last a reasonable man a lifetime, while reserving £40 for the relief of more pressing needs: nor need common sense be too consciously attended to in performing the act – these things can always, in a well-regulated mind, be done, as it were, under plain cover. Fielding drives home this point, in fact, by having Partridge, whose concern is clearly Partridge's opinion of Partridge, make a solemn offer of a guinea, which Mrs Miller sharply refuses.

But then, perhaps Tom is activated by moral magniloquence:

part of mankind, consulting only their own separate advantage, endeavour to maintain one constant imposition on others, the whole world becomes a vast masquerade, where the greatest part appear disguised under false vizors and habits; a very few only showing their own faces, who become by so doing, the astonishment and ridicule of all the rest.'

the desire for the grand, self-subduing gesture, for *greatness*? Mandeville is right, I think, to say that this passion can on occasion send men to the stake, let alone deprive them of their last £50; but such a motive cannot exist in relation to a particular act alone; it requires a context, which in Tom's case is absent: he is accident-prone, indeed, but he is not *seeking* martyrdom: no reasonably competent seeker after martyrdom would achieve it on such consistently ludicrous and, as Fielding's contemporaries would have said, 'low' pretexts.

Perhaps then, like so many gently-reared persons, Tom just cannot face the thought of children's corpses? But to say this is precisely to say that he is goodhearted, unless we have recourse to Hobbes' celebrated definition of pity: that pity is fear of my own misfortune induced by the spectacle of another's. This definition has the consequence that the more likely I am to be overtaken by a given calamity the more I pity others whom it overtakes, and this might seem to help the egoist in the present case, for Mrs Miller's cousin and his family face starvation, a fate not altogether unlikely to overtake Mr Jones. But here again the attempted explanation doesn't fit. Jones is manifestly not a fearful man, and if he did fear starvation enough to be moved to give £50 away he would fear it sufficiently to keep his £50 – or some of it – in his pocket. Context in the novel thus constrains the free flights of arbitrary postulation of motive to which the vacant scythian plains of the philosophy tutorial so seductively beckon us, and in the end there is nothing to be done but to grant Jones the motive which common sense would have granted him in the first place: namely, that he very much wants the highwayman and his family not to starve. And his subsequent transports at their recovery confirm this.

But the contextual density of the novel as a form does not entirely account for the convincingness of this episode. The other force working on Fielding's side is that, in order to establish Tom's altruism it is not necessary for him to convince us that Tom is acting out of bare fidelity to a conception of virtue which has nothing to do with distress or enjoyment.[83] Tom is

---

[83] As I have already suggested, there is located somewhere here a major dividing line between Puritanism and other versions of the Christian tradition. Puritanism is, in effect, the view that a man should want nothing but to be morally justified. Compare this with Traherne's 'Your Enjoyment of the

distressed, all right, when he offers the purse to Mrs Miller; and he is delighted when he hears of the deliverance of the highwayman and his family: the moral interest is all in the question, delighted or distressed *at what*. Context can be used to decide this question convincingly, but Fielding has already slipped out of Mandeville's grasp in the long process of argument (in the broad sense of 'argument' which I have, on one level, been trying to establish as appropriate to Fielding's sort of novel) which has, earlier in the novel, established this question as the morally important one in his readers' minds.

And, finally, I think it is the fact that this question *is*, at least from the point of view of Fielding's general theory of morals, the morally important one, which led, or rather forced, Fielding to adopt the techniques of character revelation through the ironic juxtaposition of viewpoints which we discussed in an earlier chapter. If to know what a man *is* is to know what he *wants* – what he takes pleasure in – then it is no good allowing him, as Richardson does Pamela, to indulge in putatively self-revelatory monologue. One does not need to invoke Freud or Wittgenstein to make the point that there is such a thing as self-deceit; that men edit their consciousness in order to remain ignorant of their real goals. What a man wants shows in what he does and what he says and more especially, as in the palmary case of Legrandin in *Du Côté de chez Swann*, in the tension between what he says and the circumstances in which he says it. That is why the action of Fielding's novel takes place in the public world – in the spaces between men – and not in the private inner world of consciousness.

World is never right, till you so Esteem it, that every thing in it, is more your Treasure, than a King's Exchequer full of Gold and Silver' (*Centuries* I. 25) and the following:

'Socrates was wont to say, *They are most happy and nearest the Gods that need nothing*. And coming once up into the Exchange at Athens, where they that Traded Asked him, What will you Buy; what do you lack? After he had Gravely Walkt up into the Middle, spreading forth his Hands and turning about, *Good Gods*, saith he, *who would have thought there were so many Things in the World which I do not want* . . . Socrates, perhaps being an Heathen, knew not that all things proceeded from God to Man, and by Man returned to God: but we that know it: must need All things as God doth that we may receive them with Joy, and live in His Image.' (*Centuries*, I. 40.)

7

JONATHAN WILD:
THE LOGIC OF SELF-SUFFICIENCY

I

Perhaps the most obstinate myth about Fielding is the myth of his geniality: Fielding the jolly fellow, the whitewasher of minor imperfections, the bringer-in of implausible happy endings with three cheers and a bumper all round before the curtain comes down and we are left to make what we can of reality (which is not comic) amid the cigarette-ends and faded plush of the auditorium.

But even here there have been occasional murmurs of eminent dissent. Coleridge, always the odd man out, likened Fielding to Swift, and thought the chapter on hats in *Jonathan Wild* better than anything in *A Tale of a Tub*. And I think Coleridge was right. No doubt at first sight Fielding does not seem to be your man for *saeva indignatio*. But look more closely and you find that he is full of savage pessimism about the goodness of men and society which rises at times, as for example it does in the opening passages of *A Voyage to Lisbon*, to horror. Here is his description of his experiences while being carried aboard the ship at Rotherhithe.

I think, upon my entrance into the boat, I presented a spectacle of the highest horror. The total loss of limbs was apparent to all who saw me, and my face contained marks of a most diseased state, if not of death itself. Indeed, so ghastly was my countenance, that timorous women with child had abstained from my house for fear of the ill consequences of looking at me. In this condition I ran the gauntlope (so, I think, I may justly call it) through rows of sailors and water-men, few of whom failed of paying their compliments to me, by all manner of insults and jests on my misery. No man who knew me will think I conceived any personal resentment at this behaviour; but it was a lively picture of that cruelty and inhumanity, in the nature of men, which I have often con-templated with concern, and which leads the mind into a strain of very uncomfortable and melancholy thoughts. It may be said, that this barbarous custom is peculiar to the English, and of them only to the lowest degree; that it is an excrescence of an uncontrolled licentiousness mistaken for liberty, and never shows itself in men who are polished and refined, in such manner as human nature requires, to produce that perfection of which it is susceptible, and to purge away that malevolence of disposition, of which, at our birth, we partake in common with the savage creation.[84]

This vein of indignant pessimism dominates in *Jonathan Wild*, and in the essay on *The Characters of Men*. And once you have encountered it there and acquired an ear for the ironic mode in which this side of Fielding expresses itself, you can trace it, running like some dark and heavy polar current, beneath the sunlit geniality of *Tom Jones*. Tom moves through a world in which men are commonly as feeble as they are vicious, in which lust, fraud, nepotism, arrogance, witless intemperance and cold-blooded cruelty govern society from the secret chambers of great men; in which vice and hypocrisy naturally flourish, and kindness, honour and decency go more often than not to the wall.

Such a pessimism makes short work of Butler's comfortable assurance that virtue and self-interest go hand in hand. But the more one opposes goodness to self-interest, the more apparently one is left confronting Butler's question: Why should a man be moral? Why should we open ourselves to commitments, to pleasures, desires, duties, which on Fielding's own account largely disable the man who is subject to them from pursuing his own interests like a rational being? Do we really want to end up like Tom, who regularly forgets all about maximising his gratifications, or establishing a sensible balance of present and future pleasures, in his foolhardy haste to save Mrs Waters or the Man of the Hill from armed assailants, or to bestow all his worldly goods upon a virtuous highwayman, or to give himself up to sottish rejoicing at his benefactor's recovery when prudent sobriety and a sharp eye to Blifil's weak points would better suit his condition?

Looked at from a philosophical point of view these are very

[84] *A Voyage to Lisbon*, entry for June 26, 1754.

odd and peculiar questions. One wants to say, perhaps, that anyone who asked them *seriously* would by his very seriousness in asking them have put himself beyond the possibility of receiving a serious answer to them. After all, the reason why a man feels morally required, say, to jump into a weir to save a drowning child is, simply, that the child is drowning. Of course this is uninformative from the point of view of a man who can seriously ask, Why should I be moral? *He* wants to know why one should bother to save drowning children. But as long as he persists in taking the standpoint of an outsider, of one to whom morality is a mystery, it will be impossible to explain the mystery to him. It will be no use talking to him of the child's fear, of a life cut short, of the feelings of the child's parents, and so on, for if he does not see the force of moral claims *in general* he will, *a fortiori*, fail to see the force of *these* moral claims, just as he failed to see the force of the moral claim presented by the drowning child in the first place.

The man who does feel the force of the moral claim presented by the drowning child, of course, needs no further reason for responding to it beyond the simple fact that the child is drowning. In fact, if you were to ask an ordinary, inarticulate, straightforward sort of man why he jumped into a weir to save a drowning child he would most likely, I think, first fail to understand the drift of your questioning, and then, perhaps with some irritation, say something to the effect that *he had to do it*, or that *nobody could have done otherwise*.

And this again seems very odd. It now looks as though the ordinary, unreflective moral man is acting *under compulsion*, as though he is *in the grip of an impulse*, perhaps even a *slave to his impulses* (notice how the language is getting more extreme) who has abandoned any attempt to *bring his behaviour under the control of his will*. If we go on like this we may even manage to whip up in ourselves a real *frisson* of horror at the moral man's condition: he has abandoned self-control; he is in the grip of forces which may lead him anywhere.

But here we should draw back and try to recover our grip on that sense of reality which, as Bertrand Russell somewhere wisely observes, is indispensable to a mind engaged in abstract philosophical speculation if it is not to be led up inviting garden-paths of plausible reasoning into hopeless absurdity. It is more likely to be our philosophical impulses than the unreflective virtuous man's moral ones that are at fault. For it is simply absurd to say that a man who jumps into a weir to save a drowning child is, because he requires no further reason for doing this than that the child is drowning, a *slave to his impulses*, or in general a *weak willed* or *unthinking man.* Indeed such a man might well have to conquer a momentary but very well grounded impulse of aversion to leaping into such treacherous water in order to do the deed. The only respect in which the unreflective moral man is similar to a man in the grip of an impulse, in fact, is that the moral man, like the impulsive man, habitually allows one desire or class of desires automatic precedence over any other consideration whatsoever. He does not need to *think*, in the sense of *calculating the consequences*, as he leaps into the weir, because he is leaping in the service of a type of impulse which, in his scheme of ends, habitually takes precedence over any other impulse, and thus automatically takes precedence over any other impulse that he might happen to feel at this particular time.

Seeing this, we can see more clearly, I think, what exactly it is that is so odd about the question, Why should I be moral? One could only ask such a question if one regarded *all* considerations as bargaining counters to be weighed against one another from the point of view of self interest. There is an obvious sense, of course, in which a man who can take such a stand is more his own master than a moral man. The moral man has surrendered in advance, as it were, the *perfect* freedom to decide whether, and how, to act on certain types of impulse: the systematically self-interested man has not. Hence the systematically self-interested man is in one sense out of the power of other people: they have no power to compel him to act by presenting him with unavoidable moral claims. In that sense he is self-sufficient. Butler and Hobbes, curiously enough, although their theories of morals appear on the surface so radically different, both write from the point of view of this kind of moral self-sufficiency. Hobbes, in effect, considers it the natural and inevitable condition of mankind; while Butler, as we have seen, elevates it to a curious kind of parity with morality, by treating desire for the good of others as a mere *particular passion*, something which, because it is a passion, has nothing essentially to do with morality, morality having to do with the establishing of an order or ranking among the passions by reference to some principle of choice.

The image of man as morally self-sufficient thus confronted Fielding in the philosophy of his age in two forms, a black, or sceptical form, in Mandeville and Hobbes and a white (or rather whitewashed) form in the work of Butler and other respectable benevolist writers. From both directions the nagging question recurs: Why be like Tom? Why not be morally self-sufficient? Is not self-sufficiency more in your interest?

II

To this question Fielding has an answer. It can be worked out from an intelligent reading of *Tom Jones* but it is most clearly and forcibly presented in *Jonathan Wild*. The historical figure of Wild serves Fielding as an example of a character more often to be met with in philosophical discussion than in fiction: the man who practises absolute moral self-sufficiency; who brings every consideration without exception before the bar of self-interest.

What I with academic lameness have called moral self-sufficiency Fielding calls, with capitals, GREATNESS. *Jonathan Wild* is a satire upon GREATNESS and GREAT men. What is impressive, to me at least, about the book, is its combination of a dry, disenchanted, forensic exposition of the everyday mechanics of successful villainy with something much more interesting and morally profound: an overpowering vision of the desolation, vacuity and death of spirit on which these neat clicking mechanisms feed and to which they lead. Fielding has breathed a dreadful life into the *Newgate Calendar* and turned it into a vision of hell.

Wild, like his original, is the leader of a gang of thieves. They rob on his instructions. He keeps most of the booty, and in addition carries on an open or 'front' business as a 'thief-taker'; that is he 'recovers' stolen property and sells it back to the rightful owner, and he delivers thieves to justice. These are on occasion members of his own gang who have rebelled against his control or held back loot for themselves: he suborns witnesses against them and they duly hang. 'This double method of cheating the very tools who are our instruments to cheat others,' says Fielding, 'is the superlative degree of greatness, and is probably, as far as any spirit crusted over with clay can carry it, falling little short of diabolism itself.'[85]

A man in Wild's position must be self-sufficient if he is to survive at all. His situation forces him into a radical dependence upon his own wits, quickness of action and force of character. He must always know more and know it sooner than those beneath him. He must never hesitate to use his superior knowledge to establish his supremacy by playing off one member of the gang against another, or legal against criminal society; and this supremacy must be constantly reestablished every hour of every day. He can thus never allow himself to relapse into relying at any point on the undeceived goodwill of another human being: no relationship is open to him which is not in its very essence based upon the acknowledged or unacknowledged possibility of betrayal at the first opportunity which seems convenient. Although surrounded by other men, Wild is as alone as that other great fictional exponent of solitary self-sufficiency, Robinson Crusoe.

Fielding sees, what is obvious, that this is an unenviable situation. Wild's pleasures are few and their enjoyment uncertain. His life is a continual turmoil of plotting and counterplotting. His mistress, Laetitia Snap, is an avaricious whore who gluts her vanity with a foppish attorney's clerk, Tom Smirk, her sexual appetites with Bagshot, one of Wild's own thugs, and reserves for Wild such favour as she can make him pay for. So far, Fielding seems in accord with Butler in holding, roughly speaking, that the answer to the question 'Why should I be moral?' is that immorality does not lead in practice to a satisfactory balance of happiness over unhappiness in the long run.

This answer is a feeble and unsatisfactory one, it seems to me. It shows, perhaps, why I should not devote myself to organised crime on a Wildean scale, but it does not show why I should not grind the faces of my employees, browbeat my wife, or take a bribe or two of the safer sort if such activities can, as they often can, be combined with a generally respectable and relatively invulnerable life. An adequate answer to the question Why

[85] *Jonathan Wild*, Book 2, Chapter 2.

should I be moral? should bear not just upon extreme wickedness but on the comfortable peculations of everyday life.

Here, I think Fielding shows his genius. First of all, and
rather plausibly, he makes Wild recognise the miseries and un-
certainties of his life, *and stick to it in spite of them*, in implicit
defiance of Butlerian prudence.

Wild, finding his search ineffectual, resolved to give it over
for the night; he then retired to his seat of contemplation, a
night-cellar, where, without a single farthing in his pocket,
he called for a sneaker of punch, and, placing himself on a
bench by himself, he softly vented the following soliloquy:

'How vain is human GREATNESS! What avail superior
abilities, and a noble defiance of those narrow rules and
bounds which confine the vulgar, when our best-concerted
schemes are liable to be defeated! How unhappy is the state
of PRIGGISM! How impossible for human prudence to
foresee and guard against every circumvention! It is even as
a game of chess, where, while the rook, or knight, or bishop,
is busied in forecasting some great enterprise, a worthless
pawn interposes and disconcerts his scheme. Better had it
been for me to have observed the simple laws of friendship
and morality than thus to ruin my friend for the benefit
of others. I might have commanded his purse to any degree of
moderation: I have now disabled him from the power of
serving me. Well! but that was not my design. If I cannot
arraign my own conduct, why should I, like a woman or
child, sit down and lament the disappointment of chance?
But can I acquit myself of all neglect? Did I not misbehave
in putting it into the power of others to outwit me? But that
is impossible to be avoided. In this a *prig* is more unhappy
than any other: a cautious man may, in a crowd, preserve his
own pockets by keeping his hands in them; but while the *prig*
employs his hands in another's pocket, how shall he be able
to defend his own? Indeed, in this light, what can be
imagined more miserable than a *prig*? How dangerous are
his acquisitions! how unsafe, how unquiet his possessions!
Why then should any man wish to be a *prig*, or where is his
greatness? I answer, in his mind: 'tis the inward glory, the
secret consciousness of doing great and wonderful actions,

which can alone support the truly GREAT man, whether he be a CONQUEROR, a TYRANT, a STATESMAN, or a PRIG. These must bear him up against the private curse and public imprecation, and, while he is hated and despised by all mankind, must make him inwardly satisfied with himself. For what but some such inward satisfaction as this could inspire men possessed of power, wealth, of every human blessing which pride, avarice and luxury could desire, to forsake their homes, abandon ease and repose, and at the expense of riches and pleasures, at the price of labour and hardship, and at the hazard of all that fortune hath liberally given them, could send them at the head of a multitude of *prigs*, called an army, to molest their neighbours; to introduce rape, rapine, bloodshed, and every kind of misery among their own species? . . . Lastly, what less inducement could persuade the *prig* to forsake the methods of acquiring a safe, an honest, and a plentiful livelihood, and, at the hazard of even life itself, and what is mistakenly called dishonour, to break openly and bravely through the laws of his country, for uncertain, unsteady, and unsafe gain? Let me then hold myself contented with this reflection, that I have been wise though unsuccessful, and am a GREAT though an unhappy man'.[86]

Self-interest in the ordinary sense has ceased, paradoxically enough, to be Wild's dominating motive. What has replaced it is pride in his own absolute self-sufficiency; in the naked power of his will to conquer all obstacles merely for the sake of conquering them. He is sustained by a kind of black, or inverse, puritanism. The puritan is one who will not follow a multitude to do evil. He demands of himself an absolute moral authenticity, and locates such an authenticity in his own inner power to cleave, by an act of will,[87] to a set of moral principles conceived as having unconditional authority irrespective of consequences. In pursuit of authenticity he separates himself from other men as Christian does from the family he leaves behind in the City of Destruction, or an actual Puritan, Roger Williams, did from

[86] *Op. cit.*, Book 2, Chapter 4.

[87] It is Pamela's frequent boast, in Richardson's novel, that although she is poor in all else, she is rich in *will*.

the congregation he considered, one by one, to be no longer fit to pray with him. Moreover the moral principles to which the puritan owes his absolute allegiance cannot be justified *as* moral principles by the contribution which their observance makes to human happiness, for to say that would be to imply that our observance of them constitutes a *moral* claim on God's mercy. But – and this is a central doctrine of the Reformation, and especially of Calvinism – we cannot regard salvation as something to which any creature has a moral right accruing to him from his works. It is a free and absolute gift of God's will. And therefore the rectitude which the puritan demands of himself is a willed and unswerving obedience to God's will merely because it is God's will.

We know from many places in Fielding's work his low opinion of the doctrine of salvation by grace and of the unnecessariness of good works to salvation. Wild's 'inward glory, the secret consciousness of doing great and wonderful actions' which buoys him up in the midst of the vilification and misfortune which is the lot of the prig (thief) is the mirror image of the inner satisfaction in his own justification which buoys up the puritan in his not dissimilar isolation. Both have chosen to found their lives upon the integrity of the solitary will and to abandon if necessary all human relationship in the service of that ideal. The only difference is that the puritan defines the integrity of his will in terms of obedience to the will of God, while Wild defines it in terms of obedience to the demands of his own appetites. And this makes less *moral* difference than one might suppose, given that, for the puritan, God's will is to be obeyed not because it is good by any standard of goodness external to it but merely because it is God's will. In some puritan writings it is almost as if the value of God and morality alike were simply that they make possible the puritan practice of integrity of will: and this, after all, is the modest role which Wild ends by assigning to his appetites. In the end they are inessential, for in the end Wild wants nothing in the world but to be great, just as the puritan wants nothing in the world but to be justified.

GREATNESS in short, has no content. To desire to be GREAT is not to pursue any positive object of desire; it is to desire to be able to do without all positive objects of desire.

Wild despises the 'vulgar', who need affection, trust, the pleasures of children, and so on: it is his boast that he needs nothing (but GREATNESS).

To be in this condition, Fielding thinks, is to be automatically cut off from morality, for to be in the world of morality, and open to moral claims, just is a matter of habitually pursuing certain objects of desire: the good of friends or children, the integrity of one's relationships with them, and so on, and so on. Because Wild pursues only GREATNESS all the experiences, emotions and gratifications which go with morality are a closed book to him: like Blifil and his uncle he pulls the wool over his own eyes with self-defeating cynicism.

> To this silly woman did this silly fellow [Heartfree] introduce the GREAT WILD, informing her at the same time of their school acquaintance with the many obligations he had received from him. This simple woman no sooner heard her husband had been obliged to her guest than her eyes sparkled on him with a benevolence which is an emanation from the heart, and of which great and noble minds, whose hearts never swell but with an injury, can have no very adequate idea, it is, therefore, no wonder that our hero should misconstrue as he did, the poor, innocent, and simple affection of Mrs Heartfree towards her husband's friend, for that great and generous passion, which fires the eye of a modern heroine, when the colonel is so kind as to indulge his city creditor with partaking of his table to-day, and of his bed to-morrow. Wild, therefore, instantly returned the compliment as he understood it, with his eyes, and presently after bestowed many encomiums on her beauty, with which perhaps she, who was a woman, though a good one, and misapprehended the design, was not displeased any more than the husband.[88]

We can thus reconstruct as follows Fielding's reply to those who think that the question 'Why should I be moral?' offers a pressing philosophical problem. If I care at all for the good of others then I am within the realm, or the conceptual universe, of morality, and subject to moral claims, and thus the question is an idle one from my point of view. It amounts for me simply to the question 'Why should I do x?' or 'Why should I refrain

[88] *Op. cit.*, Book 2, Chapter 1.

from doing y?' where what makes x a good and y a bad action is sufficiently obvious to me, given that, *ex hypothesis*, I understand and feel the force of moral claims. Like Tom, I may backslide, but not without feeling and suffering inwardly for it.

The question must therefore be rephrased as, 'Why should I put myself in the position of feeling, and so being subject to, moral claims? Wouldn't I be better able to pursue my own interests if I were insensible to the force of moral claims and distinctions?' And here the power of Fielding's imagination in *Jonathan Wild* comes into play. For what Fielding is saying, in effect, is that it is not intelligible to suppose that I can further my *interests*, in the sense of maximising my satisfactions, by placing myself outside morality and making myself insensible to its claims. For what overtakes me if I try to do this, as it overtakes Wild, is what can only be described as a sort of motivational anaemia. Wild has no emotional ties with other people; therefore he can have none of the motives which spring from such ties – of friendship, civic pride, domestic affection, political loyalty, and so on – and hence none of the pleasures which spring from the satisfaction of such motives. What he is left with is a restricted set of bodily needs and the pleasures of malice and revenge. These offer enjoyments too feeble and uncertain to sustain him for long: therefore he is thrown back on GREAT-NESS, which is not a goal, but an apotheosis of goal-lessness; an empty glorying in the ability to do without. The attempt to satisfy one's positive appetite more richly by opting out of morality thus ends in a life sustained, paradoxically enough, by nothing but the desire to rise superior to one's appetites in the exercise of an autonomy of will which has for its object not even the puritan's or ascetic's goal of salvation, but merely its own existence, which is to say: nothing. The real horror about Wild's greatness, and it is a horror which Fielding transfers, through the book's dimension as a political satire, to all pursuit of greatness through aggression and domination, is not that it is wicked but that it is vacuous. The great man, in Proust's phrase, is a sculptor of nothingness: his greatness is not even a word, but a corrupt misuse of a word, and it conceals not the achievement but the abandonment of all real and positive human goods.

I find this a powerful and terrible vision, and so far as I know it is original to Fielding. Many philosophers, including Plato and Shaftesbury, have held that the immoral man suffers as a result of his immorality, through being the slave of passions like anger, suspicion and fear which are as destructive to the mind subject to them as to those about him. But the vision of the flight from morality as culminating in the abandonment even of appetite in the service of an empty self-sufficiency is Fielding's own. Fielding was searching here, it seems to me, towards an insight of great power and generality: that the universe of significations within which an individual man can frame an intelligible life for himself, and even formulate the conditions of his own private happiness, is not a universe which exists for the individual man separated from society and from those psychologically intrinsic, and not merely political or commercial, relationships with other men which constitute the field upon which moral distinctions define themselves.[89] This is not a very English insight: at least it is not a very Whiggish insight, and English philosophy has characteristically been a Whig philosophy. But then, it is because his thought is set so obstinately against the thought of his time, which is in many ways also our time, that I find Fielding such an interesting writer.

[89] The reader should not suppose me to be claiming, that is, that the avoidance of 'motivational anaemia' is, or could be, a *motive for being moral*: it could not be, because the state of mind resulting from such a 'choice' of morality would not, *ex hypothesi*, be a moral one. My point, or rather what I take Fielding's point to be, is simply that the man who proposes to serve his *interests* better by opting out of morality is formulating an incoherent and self-defeating intention: Wild is abandoning 'interest' along with 'morality', and opting instead for greatness, which is itself neither, but rather the evacuation of both.

BIBLIOGRAPHY

1 Text

Tom Jones, the greatest work of Fielding's maturity, appeared in February 1749, seven years after the publication of *Joseph Andrews*, and six years before Fielding's untimely death in 1755 at the age of forty-seven. It was produced by Fielding's publisher, Andrew Millar, in six duodecimo volumes. Despite the vilification to which Fielding was ceaselessly subjected by political and literary opponents, the book enjoyed an immense and immediate popular success, running in the course of 1749 alone through four London editions and one Dublin edition. Millar had initially paid Fielding £600 for the copyright, but later added another £100 in view of the book's huge sale.

2 General and Biographical

M. P. Willcocks, *A True-Born Englishman* (Allen & Unwin), 1947, is a good readable biography of Fielding. Longer biographical-cum-critical studies are: Aurelian Digeon, *The Novels of Fielding* (Russell and Russell, N.Y.), 1925, reissued 1962, and Frederic T. Blanchard, *Fielding the Novelist* (Yale University Press, New Haven), 1926. F. Homes Dudden, D. D., *Henry Fielding, His Life, Work and Times* (Oxford University Press), 1952, 2 volumes, 1183 pp., is exhaustive and fascinating.

3 Critical Books

On Fielding's irony: Glenn W. Hatfield, *Henry Fielding and the Language of Irony* (University of Chicago Press 1968, and Eleanor N. Hutchens, *Irony in 'Tom Jones'* (University of Alabama Press). On Fielding's moral outlook, especially as this bears upon his latitudinarian moral theology: Martin C. Battestin, *The Moral Basis of Fielding's Art: A Study of 'Joseph Andrews'* (Wesleyan University Press) 1959. On the problems of technique in the novel discussed in Chapters 2 and 3: Gabriel Josipovici, *The World and the Book* (Macmillan, Stanford University Press), 1971.

4 Articles

Frank Kermode, 'Richardson and Fielding', *Cambridge Journal*, 4 (1950), 106–14.

William Empson, 'Tom Jones', *Kenyon Review*, XX (Spring 1958), 217–49.

Eleanor N. Hutchens, '"Prudence" in *Tom Jones*, A Study of Connotative Irony', PQ XXXIX (1960), 496–507.

John Middleton Murry, 'In Defense of Fielding', in *Unprofessional Essays*, (Jonathan Cape), 1956.

5 Collections of Critical Articles

A great deal of eighteenth-century criticism, some of it of great interest, is assembled in: Ronald Paulson and Thomas Lockwood, eds., *Henry Fielding, The Critical Heritage* (Routledge), 1969. Some of this is also to be found in: Neil Compton, *Henry Fielding, Tom Jones: A Casebook* (Macmillan), 1970, which also contains some recent articles, including those by Empson and Murry listed above.

6 *The Philosophical Background*

Basil Willey, *The English Moralists* (Chatto & Windus, Norton, N.Y.), 1964, and Leslie Stephen, *History of English Thought in the Eighteenth Century*, volume II (Rupert Hart-Davis, Harcourt Brace Jovanovich, N.Y.), 1962, offer the best introduction to the moral philosophy of the period for the reader who is not a technical philosopher. There are good discussions of Butler in C. D. Broad, *Five Types of Ethical Theory* (Routledge, Humanities Press, N.Y.) 1930. Austin Duncan-Jones, *Butler's Moral Philosophy* (Penguin). Shaftesbury's *Characteristics* is available in a Library of Liberal Arts paperback edition. All the British moralists discussed here can be found in ruthlessly abridged versions in D. D. Raphael, *British Moralists*, 1650–1800, volume I, (Oxford) 1969, and at greater length in Selby-Bigge, *British Moralists* (Library of Liberal Arts), 1964, which remains the standard anthology. Kant's moral philosophy is best studied in H. J. Paton's excellent annotated translation, *The Moral Law* (Harper & Row, N.Y.).

Randall Library – UNCW

NXWW

PR3454.H7 H28

Harrison / Henry Fielding's Tom Jones : the noveli

304900221956+